A Twenty-First Century Seeker

A Twenty-First Century Seeker

Seeker

maintaining spiritual principles
in a very hectic world

Pradhan Balter

Blue Beyond Books

ISBN 978-0-9957531-0-5

Blue Beyond Books Limited
4 Paget Road, Ipswich
IP1 3RP, United Kingdom

www.bluebeyondbooks.co.uk

Printed in the Czech Republic.

My Prayer and Gratitude

Please allow me to acknowledge that it is only by the Grace of the Supreme, and my Guru's love, that I have anything of worth to say or write. I do hope that in the pages that follow, you will find some joyful inspiration. But even if all the wisdom and knowledge of time were placed in words, they would have no value at all if they were not endowed with love. I pray to the Supreme that the words in this book will be blessed with a drop of His unconditional Love.

— *Pradhan Balter*

Acknowledgements

It was more than 25 years ago that I asked my spiritual Teacher, Sri Chinmoy, if I could write a book about my experiences with him. "Do it, do it!" came the reply. My heart of gratitude goes to my Guru. Without his loving encouragement, I would have nothing to write.

Many of my friends encouraged me in this process and to all of them I say, "Thank you." Thank you to Aditi who so long ago suggested I write a book and then forced the task upon me by videotaping and transcribing, word-for-word, a series of four talks that I offered in California. Those talks ultimately served as the starting point for this book. Thank you to Priyadarshan for his non-stop enthusiasm and objective critiquing during the 16 years it took me to write; thanks to all those at Blue Beyond Books and the Golden Shore Publishing who decided that the book should have a larger audience, and took it upon themselves to make it anew: Abhisar, Pataka, Pragya, Sanjaya; and finally, to so many seekers who came to classes, asked questions and so kindly shared their spiritual aspiration with me. They have played a most significant role in my own spiritual growth.

CONTENTS

Nearly every personal introduction starts the same way:

"Bernard?"

"Excuse me?"

"I'm sorry. I didn't quite catch
your name..."

I understand. Pradhan is not
Steve, Dave, Jim or Bill. And the
fact that I bear an unusual name,
an Indian one at that, begs the
inevitable next question, "How
did you get that name?"

Pradhan is a given name,
bestowed upon me by my
spiritual Teacher*,
Sri Chinmoy (*Sri,
pronounced "Shree"*).

Introduction

I am grateful for it
and someday hope to live up to
its meaning: "...One who is great
inwardly on the strength of his
heart's openness to the light, to
the truth, to the supreme reality."
A lot of meaning for a little
seven-letter word, but such is the
nature of Sanskrit.

---

* *You'll note that I capitalise Teacher. For
me, this is simply a matter of respect, much
as one might capitalise Reverend or Rabbi.
Eastern tradition often uses the term Master,
i.e., spiritual Master, instead of spiritual
Teacher.*

Sanskrit is an ancient language that is rooted in spiritual experience. As such, there are words in Sanskrit with broad spiritual meaning and no corresponding direct English translation. It often takes many English words to define a single Sanskrit word.

My parents named me Sidney, but I was never called that. I was always called Sandy. The story goes that my name was to begin with the letter "S" according to the Jewish tradition of naming a newborn to honour someone who had recently passed. For me, that was my Uncle Sam. Apparently, the nurses woke my mother up at 4 a.m. to ask what her newborn son was to be named and she blurted out "Sidney". Now, Sidney is a fine name, but it's not what my parents had planned, especially since that was the name of my mother's boyfriend before my father. Oy!

The story continues that for two weeks there was much ado in my family about what and what not to call me. My older brother, Lenny, was one of those kids who had trouble pronouncing spaghetti ("pisghetti") and he somehow transformed Sidney into Sandy. That's what stuck. I was called Sandy until 1976, when Sri Chinmoy gave me the name Pradhan.

I was raised in the suburbs of New York City and now live in Chicago. I've earned my living in a number of professions. I practised chiropractic for three years. I have written a number of training manuals for the graphics program CorelDRAW. I now own a small and wonderful (if I do say so myself) vegetarian breakfast house called "Victory's Banner" and a flower shop called "Gratitude~Heart~Garden".*

---

*   *A quick note to American readers. Because this book is distributed in other countries, I've opted for British punctuation rules and spelling! Thus, you'll often see British spellings of words, for example,* self-realisation *instead of* self-realization.

More relevant to this book, I've been involved in yoga and the meditative life for some 47 years. Most people associate yoga with headstand and sitting in the lotus position. This aspect of yoga, "hatha" yoga, is a small branch of the yoga tree. "Yoga" is actually another Sanskrit word which means "union", union with truth or union with God. The major religions can all be thought of as branches of the yoga tree.

I've had the very good fortune to travel widely and lecture in many places, which is why my bio includes "international lecturer". (It sounds so formal, as if I should always be wearing a suit.) Perhaps the most satisfying thing about my travel-lecture experience is that I found that spiritual processing is alive and well. Regardless of the language spoken, the religion practised or the cultural differentiation, the quest for some sort of centring—for knowledge of self, for spiritual things, for peace—seems to be universally present and is a uniting force among the humankind with whom I have come in contact.

As I mentioned, I am a student of Sri Chinmoy. As of this writing, I have been his student for some 45 years. I have served as director of the Sri Chinmoy Centre in Chicago for 43 of those years. Sri Chinmoy is an Indian spiritual Teacher—a very genuine spiritual Teacher. In the East, the concept of the spiritual Teacher is well accepted and valued, but in the West, it is foreign and often misunderstood.

It would be appropriate to briefly introduce him now and explain how he fits into this introduction-to-meditation book.

Typically, when Sri Chinmoy is introduced, it is in terms of his accomplishments which, by any standard, are quite remarkable. As an author, Sri Chinmoy wrote more than 1,800 literary works on a broad spectrum of spiritual subjects. As an artist, he created more than 140,000 works of art, a collection called *Jharna-Kala*, which means "Fountain-Art" in his native Bengali language.

Creating a special genre of artwork was his avocation during the later years of his life. Sri Chinmoy considered a bird to be a wonderful metaphor for the human soul, which seeks the freedom of the Infinite. Like the caged bird, the soul is also caged in the body. In 1991, Sri Chinmoy began drawing birds, a series called *Dream-Freedom-Soul Birds.* This series numbered over 16 million works when Sri Chinmoy passed away in 2007.

The tiniest sampling of Sri Chinmoy's 15 million Dream-Freedom-Soul Birds

Sri Chinmoy was also a composer-musician. He composed some 23,000 devotional songs in both Bengali and English. He performed his own compositions on a number of instruments and offered more than 750 concerts of prayerful music around the world.

Music plays a special role in Sri Chinmoy's teachings. Music as a wordless language easily conveys feeling and, in this regard, it is very close to meditation. We readily allow music into our "inner space", to massage that inner space in a particular way. We listen to calming music to "chill", or more upbeat music when we are in need of energy. Sri Chinmoy's music is designed for that inner space. It is music created from the illumined heart and for the aspiring heart. As such, it has a deeply profound impact on the consciousness of the listener.

Sri Chinmoy was also an avid athlete, tennis player, runner and weightlifter.

But first, foremost and above all, Sri Chinmoy was a genuine man of the spirit—a man of intense prayer and meditation. At the age of 12, he and his brothers and sisters moved to the Sri Aurobindo Ashram in Pondicherry, India. Here he spent hours a day in intense spiritual consecration. Indeed, it is from this spiritual dimension that all of Sri Chinmoy's activities derived both their source and their strength.

In 1964, some 20 years later, he moved from his native India to New York City where he founded the family of International Sri Chinmoy Centres that are dedicated to spiritual study and community. More than 7,000 students around the world study meditation and practise a sincere spiritual life following Sri Chinmoy's teachings.

Sri Chinmoy in a meditative moment

At this point, I want to clarify that this is not a book on "Sri Chinmoy-ism" per se. It is, however, definitely a reflection of his impact on my life. I happily and uninhibitedly confess to you that everything that is "Pradhan", in the way of spiritual development, is a result of my encounter with Sri Chinmoy. Sri Chinmoy is more than a friend and teacher to me—my relationship with him is that of a spiritual parent and child. I am fond of saying that Beatrice and Irving gave birth to Sandy, while Sri Chinmoy gave birth to Pradhan. He is a Teacher in the true tradition—a great spiritual Teacher.

How to use this book

This book is divided into progressive sections. Each one grows from what came before it. Throughout the book are exercises for you to do. **Perform them in the course of your reading.** That is, put the book down, do the exercise and then pick the book up again.

You'll notice that throughout the book, beginning with this page, there are selected quotes from the writings of Sri Chinmoy, and occasionally references from other Teachers. (Unless stated otherwise, all of the references indicated with a 🍃 s.c., such as you see on this page, are from the writings of Sri Chinmoy.) I include these writings for a number of reasons. Frankly, I must defer to them. I am a beginner—we are all eternal beginners. The words of the evolved Teachers are infused with their consciousness, and it is from this consciousness that the words derive their power. I have chosen to sprinkle the text with inspiring quotes that relate to the subject being discussed. I find that they express even the simplest concept much more eloquently than I ever could, and I hope you find these passages as inspiring as I do.

> From the spiritual point of view, every seeker is a beginner. A beginner is he who has the inner urge to grow into something ever more divine, ever more illumining and ever more fulfilling. The moment you want to make constant and continuous progress, the moment you want to constantly surpass yourself and enter into the ever-transcending Beyond, at that moment you become an eternal beginner. 🍃 s.c.

Most of the great Teachers refer to God. I believe in God, a very interactive God at that. But I was not always that way and you need not believe in God to use this book. In fact, when I first started my own study, I had satisfactorily proven to myself that

God could not exist. The universe was just too big. The major influence in my own transition from a non-believer to a believer was, and remains, my interaction with Sri Chinmoy, who spoke constantly, devotedly and consistently about a very personal God—a God as Father, Mother, Friend, Inner Pilot and Companion. My own life experience and meditation now reinforces this belief.

As I stated, you need not believe in God to use this book or to meditate. But you will need, at least, a willingness to explore your own inner environment.

Allow me to share a personal experience that I had with Sri Chinmoy. In 1991, I received an interesting response from him to a question I had asked. About 100 students were in Bali with Sri Chinmoy for a winter holiday retreat. Sri Chinmoy gave a very inspiring talk about how "love of God" was the cornerstone of his spiritual path. During this talk, every other sentence mentioned "love of God". Guru* was speaking from a high meditative conscious-ness and his words were infused

> "The Supreme never demands my belief in Him before He has given me evidence, infinitely more than necessary, upon which I can found my implicit faith. If I want to doubt Him, He has given me abundant opportunity to do so. Verily, here lies the magnanimity of His Compassion-Light for me. ᙥ s.c.

with the power of his meditation. After this talk, as is often the case, Guru asked if we understood and if we had any questions.

I raised my hand. "It's just two small things, Guru," I said. "It's this thing called 'love' and this thing called 'God.' I really don't know how to love very well, no less loving God!"

---

*   Sri Chinmoy is affectionately called "Guru" by his students, admirers and friends. Guru means Teacher.

He responded, "All right, you say you do not know how to love God. But certainly you have an appreciation for some aspect of God—for example, peace?" I nodded in agreement. "Then everywhere you go, in everything you do, cultivate your appreciation for peace," he added. "Try to see and feel peace everywhere. Nurture peace in your meditation. Serve peace in your life. Inside your sincere appreciation for peace will grow a spontaneous love of God, because you will see that peace is one of God's faces or one of His children. Love of God is not something you do. It is something you become."

I suspect that in regard to God, most people begin this way. While we may or may not *believe* that God exists, we know that we need more peace or more love or harmony in our lives and in the world. So, that is a perfect place to begin, with the simple recognition that we are *seeking* something that we now don't have or of which we have only a small amount.

I don't think it is important to couch everything in religious terms. In fact, many people have an aversion to the term "God" because of their associations with it from their own religious rearing. On the other hand, many readers will be perfectly comfortable with the existence of God, or perhaps the possibility of the existence of God. For this reason, whenever possible I will use a variety of terms to express the same thing. The terminology is not

> **START HERE AND NOW**
>
> Here and Now is the soul's motto. If you have not yet started, then your soul wants you to start your spiritual journey at this very moment. If you have doubt with regards to God's existence, no harm. Doubt as much as you want to. If you doubt the existence of inner peace and bliss, doubt as long as you want to. Even if you have doubts with regards to the inner life or God's reality, it is best to start your inner journey anyway. — S.C.

important. What is important, much more important, is that you practise and derive joy from the fruits of your practice. Therefore, choose the terminology that works best for you, for example, God-Realisation or Self-Realisation, God, Supreme or your Highest Self, Universal Consciousness or Omnipresent Being.

As a believer in God, I don't feel that God requires anyone to call on Him, Her or It in a specific way.

An overview

I encourage you to read this book from beginning to end, practicing the meditation techniques as you proceed. Once you have done that, you can always go back to any section to review or pull out a particular exercise or aphorism. Here is an overview.

⊙ Establishing a spiritual framework

In polling students in my classes, I find that some have never meditated before, while others are quite experienced. Most, however, fall somewhere in between. They have started and stopped and started and stopped again.

In writing this book, it is my sincere hope to provide both the inspiration and the understanding for you to develop a regular and fruitful meditative practice—regardless of your starting point. In this respect, the most important thing may be to create a motivational framework from which you can operate. And so, we'll begin with a simple analysis of what is important in our lives and the role meditation plays in creating a lifestyle that is both inwardly and outwardly fulfilling.

To support you in your process, I'll share with you the proper attitudes one should bring to meditation. In giving classes, I've noticed too many people simply seeking experience—what I call the "meditative buzz"—as opposed to recognizing the value of meditation as a self-nurturing process that should be practised regularly. This improper approach is a common reason why those new to meditation quit after a few attempts—either they feel that nothing is happening or that they are not meditating correctly. The attitude you bring to your meditation has much to do with your progress in meditating well.

I'll be introducing you to a number of different meditation techniques. Please know that if the first one should fail you for any reason, no harm—there will be many other techniques presented throughout the book. What is most important, as I mentioned earlier, is that you *perform the exercise!* To read about meditation and understand it intellectually is *not* to meditate. I could describe to you for hours on end the experience of the mango, but to really experience it, you simply have to take a bite! So, take a bite—perform the exercises.

◉ A philosophical basis for meditation

We'll explore the philosophical basis for meditation and how it fits into each of our lives. In my own life, having these under-standings served to help me sustain my meditation practice.

It's important to note that each person has a unique inner disposition and, ultimately, his or her own way of spiritual processing will be unique as well. Because our histories are all different, we may use different words to mean the same thing or alternatively, use the same word to mean different things. Therefore, it's a good idea to establish a common starting point and nomenclature.

◉ Consciousness

Central to understanding meditation and its value in our lives is a discussion on consciousness and its manifestations. You will see this word on almost every page, so it's important to understand what I mean when I use it. Life's joys, struggles and experience are all expressions of our consciousness. Of course, as you meditate, the expression of consciousness will become more and more self-evident.

> **Consciousness is the spark of life which connects each one of us with the Universal Life.** s.c.

⊙ The basics of meditation

After you have performed a few techniques to give you a glimpse of meditation, we'll formalise the process to broaden both your understanding and experience. We'll take you step-by-step from the ABCs to the XYZs of meditation and provide many hints to make your meditation more fulfilling.

⊙ A meditative lifestyle

Most people have the anticipation that meditation will bring them some sort of inner peace, some "peace of mind". (Peace from mind may be more accurate!) In fact, when I poll people in classes as to what they hope to gain from meditation, it runs the gamut from "lowering their blood pressure" to "communion with God". But the most common reason people seek meditation is that they hope to gain some measure of peace. And it is true, properly performed meditation and properly motivated meditation will certainly create a sense of peace.

In every class I ask how many people feel that peace is important in their lives and in the world, and unanimously people agree it is important. Then I ask if love is important in their lives and in their world and again the response is a unanimous "yes". (These are not frivolous questions, as you'll see later on.)

But frankly, if anyone believes that they can meditate for 5 minutes or 10 minutes or 20 minutes in the morning and then "party down" the rest of the day with the *sincere* expectation that peace will enter into their lives—forget it, it just won't happen.

What you'll discover is that with regular meditation, your life becomes re-prioritised from the inside out. The inner life and the outer life are connected. Ultimately, you cannot separate your state of being from your state of doing. Your inner life and your outer life are intimately entwined.

There are many things that you can do outwardly to help yourself inwardly and, likewise, there are many things that you can do inwardly to help yourself outwardly. I refer to the incorporation of these outer life habits as "living a meditative lifestyle". We'll explore how this relationship happens—how meditation will affect you from the inside-out and how you can improve your meditation from the outside-in.

Again, in order to understand how meditation is going to affect you, you have to know what makes you the person you are. We are wonderfully complicated individuals. Most people are comfortable with the fact that we, as humans, are *multi-tiered*. We readily talk about our minds, our bodies, our hearts. We'll explore these tiers and show how meditation will affect each one and in so doing, encourage a kind of holistic meditation, meaning that you meditate on every level of your being.

◎ Merging the inner and outer worlds

A lot of people approach meditation with the idea, "I've just got to escape." It doesn't happen. In fact, the more one meditates, the more one usually feels the necessity of interacting with the world. If you anticipate that meditation will help you develop some sort of inner peace, some sort of inner joy, some sort of inner power, some sort of inner poise—you're absolutely correct. These things will come to you if you have the right motivation and the right approach toward your meditation. And, when you feel these things in your meditation, you will realise them as an inner wealth—a wealth that provides you with utmost satisfaction *only when you share it.*

Imagine how difficult it is to feel satisfied with an unlimited feast at your disposal when everyone around you is starving. Well, meditation will provide an inner feast. Simultaneously, your identification with humanity's inner hunger will increase, and with that comes an increased inner urgency to be of service to the world.

In the beginning, your meditation at the very least will provide you with added strength to cope with the stresses of life, instead of having to run from them. But as you become more adept at your meditation, you'll begin to feel the necessity of feeding the hungry world, not necessarily by preaching about it, but simply by sharing your inner food—allowing the fruits of your meditation to percolate and permeate through your every action and breath. The more you develop yourself spiritually, the more the world will come to lean on you for strength. So, meditation is not an escape from the world. On the contrary, it is a most powerful tool to empower you in your interactions with the world.

> "The spiritual life is never an escape from reality. On the contrary, the spiritual life is the conscious and spontaneous acceptance of reality in its totality. — s.c.

Sometimes people will insist, "Well, it *is* an escape from the world, because what are you doing? You're going to your room, you're sitting by yourself." But you have to realise that you cannot give something to the world unless you first have it yourself. First things first. From one we go to many. If you want to create peace in the world, then your first obligation is to create peace in yourself. Once you've done that, then you are in the right position to give it to the world. Otherwise, all our talk about peace in the world is precisely that—just talk.

We'll also deal with the difficult reality of maintaining our sense of peace and poise while in the world. Inevitably, you'll find that it is easy to meditate in a room by yourself or with a group of like-hearted people. The more difficult part is maintaining your inner peace when you're being jostled by life's events. When you're locked in traffic, when you're in an uncomfortable life/work relationship, when your taxes are being audited—that's when it's tough. How do you interact with the outer world in such a way as to maintain your inner calm?

Happily, there is a way to do it. And not only is there a way to do it, but also you will find that the world is both a wonderful teacher and an incredible theater in which you can express your spirituality. You will find yourself looking forward to each day's adventures with new enthusiasm and clarity of understanding.

> TOUCH AND ACHIEVE
>
> When your good qualities
> Go and touch others,
> Their good qualities
> come forward
> To receive from you.
>
> S.C.

◉ A spiritual path and the role of the Master

Meditation is practical both in carrying out your day-to-day affairs and in giving overall meaning to life. Yes, I believe that life has meaning, life has purpose. If you're breathing as you read this book, you can rest assured that your life has purpose.

You'll discover that life itself is a school and we are participants in that school. Like any school, we go through different stages: elementary school, high school, college, etc. And, in the course of progressing from stage to stage, my own experience has shown me that all of us are always playing one of two roles: student or teacher. We play the role of teacher when life requires us to share our experience with others. We are students when we need new information or embark upon a previously unknown task. This schooling need not be formal. It happens even while sitting with friends, dialoguing over a cup of coffee about the latest world events. We listen, talk and constantly adjust our opinions based on new information.

This holds true for spiritual pursuits as well. History reveals to us certain individuals who have served as beacons for aspiring humanity. All these great leaders address the need for a Teacher in the course of one's spiritual development. But as I mentioned earlier, the proper role of the spiritual Teacher is often misunderstood, particularly in the West, so we'll explore what that role is. Is it necessary to have a Teacher, and how does the spiritual Teacher affect one's own personal spiritual process?

> "Human life is at once a burden and a blessing. It compels man to bear continual suffering. It gives man also a great promise of God-Realisation. — s.c.

◉ At the feet of my Master

I am a storyteller. In the final section of this book, I will share with you some intimate experiences I have had with Sri Chinmoy, as his student. Many people have told me that these stories convey more effectively the role and nature of the student-teacher relationship than all of the philosophising of the earlier pages.

◉ a21centuryseeker.com website

All of the exercises in the book are available in audio form at our website: *a21stcenturyseeker.com*. In addition, you can ask questions on your own practice and experience. There are also helpful links and references to assist you. You'll find a handy contact form to reach the author.

YOUR HEART IS ALL YOU NEED

You do not need a cave
To pray to God.
You do not need a forest
To meditate on God.
What you need, you already have
In abundant quality and quantity.
Your loving, self-giving heart
Is all you need,
And you will always have it.

S.C.

You want to learn how to meditate. Great! First, let's step back from the process of meditating for a bit. I suggest to you that the dawn of the meditation experience begins with a simple consideration of the things that give your life meaning. With today's fast-paced lifestyles, too often we don't take the time to contemplate this—either we don't have time, or perhaps we are too caught up in our life scripts.

This first exercise will take just a few minutes, but it is essential because it will provide a framework upon which everything else can be built. It requires no special skills on your part. Simply take two minutes and ask yourself this question: "What qualities will give my life a greater sense of value?"

Or another way to think of this: tomorow you will wake up with a new release: version 2 of yourself! What is

Establish a Spiritual Value System

new and improved about you? How would you choose to be if you could upgrade the current version of "you"?

Let me prime the pump with some common examples. Take, for example, love. If you felt yourself to be more loving—to be able to contribute a greater sense of goodwill and oneness to your life environment—wouldn't you feel better about yourself and your relationship to those around you? Or consider peace. If you felt more peace in your life, if wherever you went you were able to convey a sense of poise and inner dignity, again, wouldn't you feel better about yourself and your life? Clearly, love and peace are two qualities that would both enrich our lives and enable us to be better contributors to our social environment. But there are many more, so take the time to do this exercise now.

> " The inner life is a blossoming heart-garden. ✒ s.c.

Exercise / Establish a value system

Close your eyes and take two minutes to consider the values that give your life meaning. What is new and improved in version 2 of you? One other way to approach this. Think of those individuals who inspire you. What are the qualities that you appreciate in others? After a few minutes of inner consideration, write these qualities down on paper—do it now!

Every class I offer begins with this exercise and, as you might expect, the larger the class, the longer the list of qualities. Allow me to share some of these with you now:

Love	Integrity	Concern
Peace	Sincerity	Selflessness
Compassion	Spirituality	Courage
Joy	Purity	Power
Devotion	Forgiveness	Faith
Enthusiasm	Acceptance	Dynamism
Determination	Patience	Creativity
Beauty	Truth	Commitment
Poise	Understanding	Progress
Inner Confidence	Oneness	Transcendence
Gratitude	Surrender	Vision
Sweetness	Happiness	Clarity
Humility	Delight	
Wisdom	Goodness	

And there are many, many more. Do you see yourself as having or wanting any of these qualities? Are there some here you did not immediately consider but are ready to adopt as your own? That's quite fine.

A few observations are important. Take a careful look at the list I provided above, and at your own list. You will quickly see that all these qualities are what I call "inner" qualities. These qualities have to do with your own inner nature or personal character. They are independent of your surroundings. True, the world serves as a vehicle to express or manifest these qualities, but unless you are fortunate enough to be born with them, *it is up to you to create and develop them.*

Allow me to pose a question that is deliberately a bit confrontational. Assuming that you can identify yourself with some of the qualities on this list, how much of your day do you consciously devote to nurturing those inner qualities—90 percent of your time? 70 percent? 50 percent? 30 percent? Many of us, sadly, spend hardly any time on this, except perhaps for a few minutes of wistful wishfulness in a day.

I am sure the dilemma is not lost on you. On the one hand, we acknowledge that it is the cultivation of these inner qualities that will give us a sense of fulfilment. On the other hand, we are caught by the outer world and can't seem to find the time to nurture ourselves within. My invitation to you is to commit yourself to those things that give meaning and value to your life. Shift your percentages. In response to the previous question, if you placed yourself at 5 percent, then make it 10 percent; if you're at 20 percent, bump it to 30 percent, etc., etc.

> Everything we desperately need in the outer life breathes secretly in our inner life. ✢ s.c.

Recognize this and commit to it now. If it is your sincere hope to develop any of these qualities, *you must be proactive* in this task. It is up to you to create the time. It is time well spent, because these are the qualities that, by your own consideration, ultimately give your life meaning and value.

As I mentioned earlier, these are inner qualities—what I would call "spiritual" qualities. I invite you to not just learn how to meditate, but also to commit yourself to consciously cultivating these inner qualities in your life. Commit yourself to living a "spiritual life". Living a spiritual life simply means the conscious cultivation of the qualities that give your life meaning.

To live a spiritual life, you need not wear the garb of the monk or priest. Quite the contrary. You have a spiritual nature and a responsibility to honour it. You also have a physical nature and a responsibility to honour it. The inner life and the outer life must go hand in hand.

Once you make this commitment, you have a reason to meditate, because meditation is a tool—a most valuable tool—to nurture your inner environment.

Let us step back a moment to consider why we don't take enough time for inner nurturing. Consider this scenario. Imagine that you have just been notified that you have won an all-expense paid trip around the world. This trip will take you to every major city in the world. You will stay at the finest hotels, eat the finest foods, and that's not all! You'll also be given $1,000 daily as spending money. To sweeten the pie, your rent or mortgage will be paid while you're gone, and your job will be waiting for you when you return. And just in case it's not, you'll receive a year's salary when you get back, tax free of course, to cover you while you look for a new job.

All you have to do to claim this prize is to be at the airport at 6 a.m. the next day, ready to take your seat in First Class. (Did I mention that you will travel First Class?) But if you're a minute late, the prize goes to someone else. Assuming this is all true, what time will you arrive at the airport? If you're like most people, you won't sleep the night before. You're at the gate hours before departure. There is no way you'll miss this opportunity.

Now, instead of this scenario, what if I told you that it is really good to meditate at 6 a.m. or earlier, because at this time the surrounding world is very quiet, and it is easier to access your inner space when things are not busy around you? Do you greet this possibility with the same enthusiasm? Perhaps you would say, "yes", but if so, you are a rare breed.

You see, the outer situation constantly claims our attention. I am fond of saying that the outer world screams for attention while the inner world merely whispers for our welcomed participation. So many times I am told things such as, "I'm going to start meditating regularly as soon as this work project ends" or "as soon as I find the time". If you're saying this now, then forget it. Put this book down and return to it when you're ready.

Make the commitment here and now to start living a spiritual life... to start cultivating those qualities that you yourself decided would give your life meaning.

It doesn't take a lot of time. Just a few minutes a day in the beginning will do. Just a few minutes. Let me tempt you a bit. The prize that comes with your inner journey is far more satisfying than that fictional trip around the world!

Exercise / **Create an inner mission statement**

Write down seven qualities that appeal to you most. You may certainly borrow from the list included earlier. This will be your starting point. Make five copies of this list. Place one at the special place where you meditate (more on this later), another on the refrigerator door, one at the door where you exit your home, another in your car and one at your workplace. These lists are to serve as reminders for you of the qualities you wish to cultivate for your own betterment and for the betterment of those around you.

To make the task easier, there is a form at the back of the book for you to use. (See Appendix, page 256.)

Techniques

Throughout the book, I'll offer a variety of techniques to bring you into meditation. But a word of caution. As adults, we often jump right into the instruction set and get lost there, losing sight of what the goal is. Please be aware that there is a difference between "the technique" and "the meditation". Many people get hung up in the issue of whether or not they are performing a technique properly. This is a mistake which I call "technique syndrome". (This is an issue that comes with adulthood. Why I say this will become clear a few paragraphs down the road.)

Imagine that you are standing at the ocean shore and you want to experience the water. There are many techniques to get into the ocean. For example, some people may fearlessly run or dive into the water. Some may walk in steadily, unerringly. If you're like me, you go in up to your ankles and then run out as soon as any threatening wave comes your way! The ocean slowly draws me into it.

Clearly, there are different "techniques" to get into the water, but the technique itself is not the thing that you seek. What you seek is to experience the ocean itself. In exactly the same fashion, there are many different techniques to lead you into meditation, but the technique itself is not the goal. The goal is to experience the inner ocean—to be washed over by our own inner ocean of consciousness. The technique is only important to the extent that it gets you into the water but it is *not* the thing you are seeking.

Much more important than the technique is this: There is a common link among all those who eventually find themselves in the water. What is that link? Well, unless they were dragged or pushed in, the reason they are in the water is that they *chose* to go in—that is, the experience was important enough to them that they overcame the obstacles in the act of getting in. *They all wanted the experience of the ocean.* Similarly, this is the most important ingredient in our spiritual efforts. We must *want* to experience our inner ocean. We must develop an *inner hunger* or yearning for the experience. It is what Sri Chinmoy calls "aspiration". Indeed, when aspiration is wed with an appropriate technique, meditation becomes spontaneous and accessible. Sri Chinmoy offers a favorite aphorism of mine: "God has prepared my meal. Now I must prepare my hunger."

> Aspiration, in its simplest definition, is a lovely flame climbing Heavenward. s.c.

Nurture your heart's hunger for peace, love, light or whatever qualities speak to you most. Cultivate those qualities in your meditation. Appreciate those qualities in others. Serve those qualities in the world.

Ultimately, you will discover which techniques work best for you. As we introduce you to different techniques, feel free to explore and adapt them to best fit you. And remember, there are many techniques. It will only be natural that some may work for you while others may not. Be patient and persevere. No sincere effort will ever go unrewarded.

A little humility helps

Continuing with our ocean metaphor (which is something I use a lot), we say we're swimming in the ocean. But is that what's really happening? The ocean, should it choose, could easily swallow us up! In reality, the ocean presents itself in such a way that we're allowed to think that we're swimming in it.

Similarly, our own inner ocean is in fact much larger than we can initially anticipate. Try not to confine the experience by your anticipation of it. It is better to invite our inner ocean to present itself to us in such a way that we can joyfully swim in it.

Patience and perseverance:
A spiritual farmer

In his excellent book, *First Things First*, Steven Covey offers the following experience and poses a rhetorical question: Most high school students, and certainly most college students, know what it is to cram for an exam. You stay up all night, study the necessary reading and take the test, hopefully with passing results. Can you imagine a farmer cramming for his crop? Can you imagine a farmer staying up all night and sowing seeds with the hope of yielding a bumper crop the next day? Of course not.

There is much to be learned from the farmer. At the appropriate time, he tills the soil. The soil may be unhealthy and rock hard. But he nurtures the soil with water and fertiliser. At the right time, he plants the seeds. For some time it may appear that nothing is happening, but the farmer continues to nurture the soil with water and appropriate nutrients. Now, we know that while the farmer is doing this, a root is pushing down into the earth and a sprout is making its way up toward the surface. It is only after some time that the farmer at last has the "Aha!" experience when the sprout breaks through the surface.

> We must realise that there is only one way of acquiring infinite future possibilities. That way lies in the great power: Humility. ⚘ s.c.

Such is the way with meditation. Be like a farmer. Don't cram. Instead, take the time to plant the seeds of peace, joy and love in your heart. Nurture these with your appropriate spiritual disciplines. The task is not to get a "meditation buzz", but instead to grow a bumper crop of most beautiful flowers in your heart-garden*.

---

* *A note about hyphenated words: In his writings Sri Chinmoy made regular use of a unique literary structure—the double hyphenated noun—probably because... (cont.)*

Enthusiasm for the task:
A child walking

You may recall I suggested that technique syndrome is an "adult" issue. Here's why. Consider the infant learning how to walk. Recently I had the wonderful opportunity to experience this first hand with my niece, Madison. I spent a lot of time with her during her first year and I watched her learn to walk. At the appropriate time, her parents (playing the role of teacher) placed her on her two feet and encouraged her step-by-step to walk, until she got both the gist of the task and the strength to accomplish it. In this case, the parents knew the child's capacity long before the child did and encouraged her to walk. Apart from this, there was no instruction set. She wasn't told, "Okay Madison, first recruit your quadriceps muscle on the left and simultaneously the hamstrings muscle on the right. Now reverse." There was no language—only example and encouragement.

Needless to say, Madison did not succeed on her first attempt. How many times did she fall on her way to her first successful step? Hundreds of times, I am sure. Yet at no time did she ever say, "Hey Mom, I need a new technique", or give up the task saying, "Hey Dad, I'm going to stick with crawling, I just can't get this walking thing down." No. Instead, she simply brought her constant enthusiasm to the task, despite not knowing exactly what the goal was or how to get there.

Sri Chinmoy is always reminding us to be like a child, and this certainly holds true for learning how to meditate. You may not know exactly what the goal is, or how to achieve it, but if you bring child-like enthusiasm to the task, you are bound to

(cont.) ...a single word could not express the nuances of his inner experiences. The spiritual heart, for example, has many aspects, so Sri Chinmoy might sometimes refer to the forgiveness-heart and other times to the compassion-heart. I have adopted this literary form in my own writings, and you'll see it throughout.

succeed. In fact, no sincere effort will remain unfulfilled in the spiritual life. According to every great spiritual teaching and Teacher, it is your destiny, your birthright to know yourself spiritually.

Practise regularly: The musician

Learning how to meditate is much like playing a musical instrument—it requires daily practice. When you learn a musical instrument you have to begin with the ABCs: how to sit properly, how to tune the instrument, how the various parts are named. And if you don't practise regularly, you'll end up having to redo the same lessons over and over, which is never satisfying.

But if you practise regularly, slowly and surely, you'll start playing beautiful music. Back in the days of my impetuous youth, almost everyone played guitar. It was a simple fact of life! I learned with the *Mel Bay* book for guitar. First, I had to learn how to tune the thing, then how to place my fingers. You can't imagine my joy when I played my first song, "Yankee Doodle", on my Harmony Red Sunburst guitar! With regular practice and enthusiasm, I was playing the Beatles in no time.

> "My God, how old are You?"
> "My child, I shall tell you. But first tell Me how old you are."
> "I am just a year old."
> "My child, if you are a year old, I am one day younger than you and one day older than you; one day younger than you in imperfection and one day older than you in perfection. Give Me half the imperfection that you have and take from Me half the perfection that I have. Let us be fully equal..." s.c.

37

There's something else. Not only will you get joy from your music, but also equally important, you'll get joy observing and participating in your own progress.

Similarly, in your meditation, you also have to start with the ABCs: how to sit, how to breathe properly, where and when to meditate. In time, you'll find yourself playing sweet and simple inner music. You'll witness yourself growing in poise, peace and happiness. With regular practice, you'll enjoy playing beautiful inner music. There is, perhaps, nothing more satisfying than being a conscious participant in your own spiritual progress.

Commitment

There it is—the terrifying "C" word. It has been my experience that most Westerners have become pretty jaded about this. As a whole, we are desperately afraid to commit to anything. Perhaps we've all gotten burned a few too many times.

> Although regularity in spiritual practice may appear mechanical, it is a constant blessing from above and shows the development of some inner strength. ✲ s.c.

If that is the case, I beg you to reconsider. Commit yourself to your own self-study. There is nothing, nor will there ever be anything as fulfilling and rewarding as the discovery of your own inner and highest self!

Consider the three things that sustain us as human beings: food, breath and spirit. Interestingly, food is what we pay most attention to, but it is the least critical of the three. We can live days and weeks without eating, should necessity demand. We pay far less attention to the breath, yet it is far more critical to our lives than food. We can live only seconds or minutes without it. The most essential sustaining element is the spiritual aspect, for without it there is no life, yet we pay least attention to it.

Think of meditation as spiritual food or nourishment. Take meditation breaks as often as you would coffee breaks. Try to cultivate the feeling that even more critical than your morning breakfast is your morning meditation.

If you are thinking, "I don't have enough time to add another thing to my daily agenda!", let's nip that idea in the bud. Meditation creates time. For every minute you put into your meditation, you'll get two minutes back in the day. You'll save time because you will develop greater poise and focus. You'll save time because you will require less sleep.

Commit now to practicing your meditation every day. It requires only a few minutes, but it will pay you back a thousand-fold in life fulfilment.

We are about to embark on the first official meditation exercise, but before we do that, let's look at some basic concepts that are common to every meditation technique. There are five aspects and concepts with which you should be familiar:

1) Proper posture
2) Proper breathing
3) Quieting the mind
4) The spiritual heart
5) Inner diligence

The ABCs of Meditation

◎ Posture

No, you don't have to sit in the cross-legged lotus position, but proper meditation does require that you keep the back comfortably erect. The classic lotus posture is helpful to the extent that it keeps the back straight, but it is not essential. Your aspiration is much more important. The back need not be stiff as in the Zen posture, nor should it be too relaxed. Simply sit comfortably erect. I prefer to use the term "alert".

It is best to meditate with your shoes off, feet flat on the floor, or crossed in front of you. You can sit on the floor if you prefer. You can use a pillow or mat. But, if sitting on the floor is difficult, then by all means sitting in a chair is just fine.

Your hands can rest or be folded in your lap, or—my particular recommendation—you can fold your hands together in a prayerful position over your heart. This makes it easier to focus on the spiritual heart, which is ultimately where you want to place your inner attention.

For most exercises, your eyes should be gently open. In the early exercises, I'll instruct you to close your eyes, as initially you may find that closing the eyes helps you focus inwardly, but ultimately, you'll want to meditate with your eyes gently open. Your spiritual nature should be available to you with your eyes closed or open, yes?

Sri Chinmoy in prayerful meditation

⊙ Breathing

As you meditate, you will naturally discover your breath becomes softer and more shallow. This is correct. Some authorities suggest breathing deeply as you meditate, but this is not correct. Unless you are performing a specific breathing exercise, you don't have to pay any special attention to your breath. It will quiet on its own as your inner noise decreases.

This relationship between a quieting of the breath and calming of the inner noise is not a coincidence. In fact, you can use this relationship to help quiet a restless mind. Simply imagine a thread in front of your nose and breathe so softly that the imaginary thread hardly moves at all. You'll quickly discover that the calmer the breath, the quieter the mind.

◉ Quieting the mind

Ultimately, the highest states of meditation take place in the complete absence of the mind. This state of meditation is well beyond the achievement of the beginner in meditation. In fact, most beginners can't fathom the possibility of experiencing anything without the mind operating. (Do not concern yourself as to how this mental silence is achieved. We'll discuss it a little later on.)

For now, all you need be concerned with is calming the mind a little bit, as this makes the "listening" part of meditation easier. Don't worry if you can't make the mind completely silent. Thoughts are like fish in the ocean. You want to experience the ocean, but if every time a thought-fish passes by you follow it, you will lose sight of the ocean. The thing to do is to simply avoid being mindful of the thoughts, that is, simply ignore them. Should thoughts come, pay them no particular attention and simply let them pass through. In the beginning, think more in terms of simply turning down the volume of your mind. We'll offer a number of different techniques to quiet the mind throughout the book.

> " Inner silence is not just the absence of thoughts. No! Silence is the blossoming of our indomitable inner will. Silence is our inner wisdom-light.
>
> ❦ S.C.

A word of caution here. Beginners often get hung up because they simply can't get the mind to be quiet. An absolutely silent mind is very advanced. Let me emphasise that at this point, you simply want to calm the intense wave thoughts in the mind, bringing the mind to a little calmer place. Later you can work on achieving absolute silence.

◎ The spiritual heart

The meditation that I prescribe occurs in the spiritual heart, not the mind. The spiritual heart is not the beating physical heart. The spiritual heart is that place where you spontaneously feel love, compassion and oneness. It will serve as the focus for almost every meditation technique offered here. (If you are familiar with the yogic system of *chakras*, the spiritual heart is associated with the fourth *chakra*.) When you point to yourself, this is the location of the spiritual heart.

> The spiritual heart embodies not only the individual consciousness but also the universal Consciousness. ⸎ s.c.

Think of the spiritual heart as another room in your being. We wake up in the morning, leave our bedroom and ultimately make our way into the kitchen. In meditation, we leave the mind–room and enter into the heart-room. Okay, perhaps this is a difficult concept at this introductory stage, but don't worry. Throughout the book, you'll find many techniques to coax you into your spiritual heart, and with just a little practice, you'll be able to do this easily and regularly.

◎ Appropriate inner diligence

When you meditate, be fully committed to it. The early exercises require only a few minutes to perform. Be fully committed at this time. Do not think about your work load, or the shopping you need to do later on in the day. Nothing else, no other agenda, is important.

Assume the proper meditation posture. Then make an immediate inner pact with yourself. Tell yourself that these next few minutes are dedicated to your inner life. For these few minutes, all of your attention, inner and outer, is dedicated to your spiritual communion. Always begin with recalling and establishing your aspiration, that is, your inner hunger for the experience.

Each technique offered in this book incorporates these basics. The exercises that appear early in the book will take you through these steps in detail. In later exercises, I'll leave these basics up to you.

Meditation in the simplest sense

Have you ever wondered why the candle seems to be ubiquitous in spiritual ceremony? Actually, it's the flame. The flame is a wonderful symbol for the inner being, or soul. It emits light and it is always climbing upward. Even if you turn a candle upside down, the flame climbs upward. The flame is said to symbolise aspiration. You'll need a candle for this exercise.

At its most basic, meditation is a four-step process. The various techniques that we offer are all embellishments of these four steps but accomplish the same thing:

1) Affirm your heart's aspiration
2) Calm or quiet the mind
3) Leave the mind-room
4) Enter the heart-room.

As you are guided through these steps, you'll find that all the basic concepts are included.

Exercise / Basic candle meditation

In an appropriately quiet location (more on this later), place a lighted candle in front of you and seat yourself a comfortable distance from it, perhaps two or three feet.

(Posture) Sit comfortably erect. The back should be alert. Remember to keep the palms of both your hands over your spiritual heart in the centre of your chest.

First, simply become aware of the hands touching the chest. Try to feel their warmth. Later, this same sensation will help you "enter the heart". Take a minute or two to concentrate on your hands over your chest. Leave your hands there through-out this exercise. Gently close your eyes.

(Inner diligence) Make an inner pact with yourself. Tell yourself that these next five, seven or ten minutes are dedicated to your spiritual life, to your spiritual communion. Nothing else is more important for these few minutes. Take just one minute to feel in your heart a sincere hunger for that inner quality that "speaks" to you most—be it peace, love or God. Imagine yourself as a child in your own heart, thirsty for these qualities. Dwell in your aspiration-hunger for a minute.

(Quieting the mind) Now, invite the mind into calm. Imagine above your head a very luminous, cloudless, blue sky. It is very clear and very vast. With each gentle inhalation, imagine all the thoughts, all the images and pictures in the mind dissolv-ing upwards into this clear sky. Feel no necessity to replace the thoughts and pictures. Let your mind become softer, more formless. Eventually, imagine the mind itself dissolving upwards into the sky, leaving you with no mind or form. You might repeat to yourself, "No mind, no form, I only exist. No mind, no form, I only exist." And then, become silent.

● ● ●

Now leave the mind-room... your breathing is probably quieter now, shallower. There is no need to deepen it, but do become aware of it. As you breathe in and out, imagine that the breath is passing through your hands directly into the heart. As the breath enters, simply "ride" on the breath, leaving the mind-room and moving deeper with each gentle breath into that space just behind your hands—the heart-room.

Now establish yourself in the heart more completely. Gently open your eyes and bring all your concentration to the candle flame, and nothing else. Don't look to the left or right of the flame, or at the candle stick, only at the flame. Try to penetrate the flame with your concentration for a minute or two.

Gently close your eyes and visualise or imagine the flame just an inch behind your hands. See it perfectly still. Concentrate on it with the same intensity.

Reopen your eyes and once more concentrate on the candle flame, but this time imagine yourself drawing the flame into your heart. Try to place it as deeply in your heart as possible.

Again, close your eyes and once more see and concentrate on the flame in your heart. Remain still for a minute more. When you are ready, take a deeper breath and reopen your eyes.

The intention of this exercise is to familiarise you with and give you a little taste of meditation. I advise you not to evaluate the experience. That would be the equivalent of the toddler, after making his first solo attempt at walking, asking himself, "Well, just how did I do?" If you experience a little more quietude—perhaps the room seems calmer to you, well and good. If you felt nothing, or perhaps couldn't accomplish any of the steps, no harm. You may simply need more practice or perhaps a different technique. What is much more important is that you have started. You have begun the process of making meditation a regular part of your life.

By the way, the utterance "No mind, no form, I only exist" is the first line of Sri Chinmoy's beautiful poem called *The Absolute*. Please take a moment to read the complete poem on page 234.

More ABCs

While explaining how to perform the candle meditation exercise, I mentioned a few helpful hints. Let's formalise those now.

The exercise began with, "In an appropriately quiet location..." Having a specific and special meditation space is very helpful. Most of us have a room where we sleep and another where we eat. Well, if you have the luxury of being able to devote a room to your meditation, that's great! But perhaps a dedicated room is too much of an investment at this point. Try to locate a corner of a room or a special spot where you know you can sit quietly and not be bothered by the surrounding environment. Make that space special for your meditation. You may want to place there a nice cloth, fresh flowers and a candle. If you are inspired by a particular spiritual figure, a spiritual Teacher perhaps, then place a photo of that person there as well.

Frankly, in my home, in addition to a dedicated meditation space, I design my entire space to be spiritually inspiring. The world provides me with enough challenges. When I come home, I want to be in a place that inspires me, strengthens me and supports me, so I decorate it with my spirituality in mind.

When you have a special place to meditate, it begins to create its own vibration. If you have ever walked into a temple or church where you felt immediately elevated, then you understand this concept. An investment in prayer and meditation has been made, and the space carries that vibration. Similarly, when you meditate at the same place every time, the space itself will begin to help you. (A few absolute no-no's: Do not place your meditation space on your microwave, on a table where you eat or a desk where you work. Make it special.)

It is extremely valuable to meditate regularly and punctually. If it is your habit to have lunch at noon every day, then you'll notice an inner clock is triggered. Perhaps 15 minutes before that time, your appetite bell starts ringing.

Well, in exactly the same way, if you meditate every day at the same time, your inner appetite will start to come forward in anticipation of being fed by your meditation.

As I mentioned earlier, it is best to meditate first thing in the morning. My own practice is to wake up, immediately shower or clean up to wash off the sleep vibration, and then meditate. This is a valuable step in becoming "proactive". If I put meditation first, then I can't miss it!

If possible, meditate before 8 a.m. After this time, the earth itself becomes much more active and restless with the hustle-bustle of the day's activity. The earlier the better: 6 a.m. is an excellent time for Western seekers who live a busy life-style. Eastern teaching suggests that 3 a.m. is the best time to meditate. This time is referred to as "the Hour of God" because it is so quiet. Most Westerners only see this hour of day when they are approaching it from the night before! If you are inspired to rise early and meditate, try it occasionally. But much more important is that you create a time for regular meditation with your aspiration fully awake. Remember, in the beginning all you need is a dedicated five to fifteen minutes.

This next meditation is a very different technique. It is about invoking and nurturing a specific inner quality—gratitude.

> My own gratitude-heart 66
> Is all that matters.
>
> ✃ S.C.

Whenever Sri Chinmoy was asked the question, "If there is only one inner quality that I should concentrate on, what should that be?" he always answered, "Gratitude." Gratitude provides the most fertile inner soil upon which other inner qualities can readily grow.

Again, for the purposes of this early exercise, I will guide you through all the steps.

Exercise / The gratitude meditation

(Posture) Sit comfortably erect. Your back should be alert. Your hands may be folded in the lap or resting on your thighs, but I recommend folding your hands in front of your heart. For this exercise, let your eyes gently close.

(Inner diligence) Begin by making an inner pact with yourself. Tell yourself that these next five, seven or ten minutes are dedicated to your spiritual life, to your spiritual communion. Nothing else is more important for these few minutes. Take just one minute to feel in your heart a sincere hunger for that inner quality or concept that speaks to you most—be it peace, love or God. Imagine yourself as a child in your own heart, thirsty for these. Dwell in this hunger for a minute.

(Quieting the mind) We'll use the same technique as before. Later, you'll learn other techniques for quieting the mind. Invite your mind into calm. Imagine that above your head is a very luminous, cloudless, blue sky. It is very clear and very vast. With each gentle inhalation, imagine all the thoughts, all the forms and pictures in your mind dissolving upwards into this clear sky. Feel no necessity to replace the thoughts and pictures. Let your mind become softer, more formless. Eventually, imagine the mind itself dissolving upwards into the sky, leaving you with no mind or form. You might repeat

● ● ●

● ● ●

to yourself, "No mind, no form, I only exist. No mind, no form, I only exist." And then, become silent.

Please imagine or recall in your heart some time or some experience with which you associate a sincere sense of gratitude. Recall that experience in your heart, almost like replaying a video and, at the same time, invoke and relive the gratitude that you felt at that time. With each gentle inhalation try to make the recollection and the gratitude more intense.

Do this for one minute. Let nothing else come into your mind; let there be no other agenda.

After a minute, let go of the specific experience and simply remain with your heart's gratitude. Imagine that the sole reason you exist is to offer gratitude—to be a source of gratitude for others. This is your only occupation. With each passing breath, extend this feeling of gratitude into the space immediately in front of you. Do this for a minute or two. Then, in the same fashion, extend gratitude behind you for another minute. Then, above you and beneath you, and to either side of you.

Finally, simply let gratitude emanate from you in every direction, upward into the sky and outward toward the horizon. Remain in this space for as long as you comfortably can. Imagine that you are gratitude itself.

It's nice to bring a meditation to an appropriate closure, and we often do this by chanting. Chanting is an entire technique unto itself, but in this case, simply chant "Shanti" (pronounced shon-tee) three times aloud. Shanti is a Sanskrit word that means "peace". Chant it slowly, prayerfully and soulfully aloud, with a sense that you are invoking peace while chanting.

● ● ●

> When you end your meditation, don't be too quick to jump back into your outer agenda. Instead, consciously begin the process of linking your inner experience with your outer experience. In this case, as you slowly open your eyes, see with gratitude. Wherever your vision falls, offer your gratitude to what you see. Look out at the world with gratitude. ✔

In a class setting, I always ask what the experience of gratitude feels like. Typical responses are, "It's loving", or "It's joyful". My favorite response is that it is liberating and expansive. I find that whenever I do this meditation, all the little issues that pinch me during the day dissolve, and I expand into something sweeter.

It's interesting to note that a single genuine inner emotion, in this case gratitude, is made up of other emotions and feelings. It's as if the recipe for gratitude is ¼ cup of joy, ½ cup of love and a teaspoon of expansiveness. Such is the nature of spiritual qualities. Inside one quality, other qualities spontaneously grow. For example, there is tremendous power in genuine peace.

> My gratitude-heart
> Always knows the way.
>
> 🍃 s.c.

So in your spiritual process, begin with those qualities that spontaneously speak to you. Use your mission statement. (Did you make one? If not, perform the exercise on page 32 now!) You can use this simple meditation with any quality and inside that quality, you'll discover other qualities growing. Again, if you were unable to do this meditation, no harm. Try it a few more times to see if it comes to you, and if not, there will be many other techniques for you to try. Remember, you have your own unique inner disposition, and ultimately your way of meditating will be unique as well.

Don't be quick to judge your experience. It is worth trying it again a few times. If you can't do this exercise right now, no harm. Remember that we are just beginners and, as such, we should be patient with ourselves and our progress.

Exercise / **Meditate every morning and evening**

You can use either of the two techniques you learned in this chapter. You might use the gratitude meditation in the morning. Or take one quality from your inner mission statement and use that quality in place of gratitude. Try to feel that you are nurturing that quality in your life. During the day, try to be a conscious expression of that quality. Witness it in others. Practise it in your life interactions.

You'll come to see that this process enables you to develop your inner muscles. The more you exercise them, the stronger they will get. There is nothing—I promise you—nothing more satisfying than to watch yourself grow into the kind of person you would like to be!

In the evening, you might use the candle meditation. Alternatively, combine these two techniques into a single meditation that you use both in the morning and in the evening.

At this point, the goals are to create regularity in your practice and a wakefulness in your life of aspiration. It is better to meditate for just seven minutes with utmost purity and intensity of effort than to simply "hang out" with your meditation for a half-hour. Make your meditation pure and filled with aspiration.

When I use the term "pure", I don't mean it in the Victorian sense. I mean it more like the orange juice that advertises itself, "there is nothing in it but the orange". When you meditate with purity, your agenda should be only to nurture your heart's aspiration—not what you are going to do later, not what you didn't accomplish earlier. Only your heart's agenda should be present.

Any method of spiritual discipline
will have two inevitable
and inseparable wings:
absolute patience
and firm resolution.

S.C.

At this point, before continuing with this exploration of meditation, please allow me a digression back to the beginnings of my own spiritual processing in the late 1960s/early 1970s. This, some of you may recall, is when the whole yoga-meditation thing first became popular. There was the hippie movement, the Beatles' visit to India, and all sorts of consciousness-altering things taking place. That era was very turbulent in terms of social change in America—Nixon was president, Viet Nam was being fought "in our living rooms", Watergate was being exposed, city blocks were being burned down and drugs were in broad and popular use among young people.

A Life Crisis

I was absorbed in the drug/hippie culture, initiated by my older brother Lenny—definitely one of those emulation things. Whatever he did, I followed suit.

Those of us who were "hippies" affectionately referred to ourselves as "freaks", and I was, by any sense of the term, a freak's freak. My hair was tied not into one ponytail, but in two—one on the top of my head and one in the back. I went to the original Woodstock rock festival, a fact which seems to evoke some reverential awe from the current batch of twenty-year-olds. I wore an earring, and in 1969 that was definitely being alternative. Especially my earring—a roach clip. People actually smoked marijuana out of my ear!

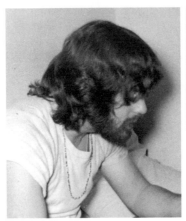

Then and now. All I can say is, "Thank God."

Okay ... I confess: I inhaled. I was a regular drug user, which included frequent experimentation with hallucinogenic drugs such as LSD and mescaline. Although I speak of my past drug usage quite casually, I wish to clarify most emphatically that ***I am not in any way, shape or form a proponent of drug use***. Quite the contrary. I can testify that although drugs may be conscious-ness-altering, they are in no way consciousness-*elevating*—a result that comes only from true spiritual pursuit.

What is relevant to this discourse, though, is that I nearly died from a drug overdose. I had unintentionally ingested an immense amount of a weird concoction of drugs that nearly killed me. Interestingly, this happened at a time when I was determined to stop taking drugs and was just getting into hatha yoga (the physical exercises).

A friend was bringing me some marijuana. Because he was late with delivery, as a token of goodwill he gave me enough of a cocaine-mescaline-speed concoction for ten people. Ironically, as I just mentioned, I intended not to have any of this concoction because of my plan to quit drugs. Later, at an afternoon party, friends coaxed me to sample a little by "snorting" it. It burned so much that we put the drug into a cola to sip on it. I can only surmise what happened. Apparently, the substance never dissolved and I must have swallowed it in a single gulp. By night's end, six of the ten people originally present fell asleep, while the remaining four sat awake in a house that fortunately was located just next to the local hospital. One of the four was severely overdosing. That was me.

Now, this was not a paranoid thing. I was a very stable drug user. I was OD-ing; there was no question about it. The experience was more than frightening at the time. I was desperately clinging to life. I could feel it. Friends took turns holding me like a baby. About eight hours into the experience, I vomited up a lot of white, undigested powder. Thank God. At this point, I felt I would be all right if I could just get to sleep. How absolutely crazy we were back in those days: to get to sleep, I took a barbiturate. I am truly fortunate to be alive.

Later, I went home and fell into a black sleep.

The next morning I awoke, still frightened, still feeling on the brink of death. My jaw was killing me from clenching my teeth. My lungs ached from hyperventilating. My parents came in, knowing something was wrong, and I told them I came home sick but was now all right. I was lying. I called my best friend and asked him to leave work to stay with me, which he did. I fell in and out of that same black sleep the entire day. Finally, I awoke at about 5 p.m., feeling, at last, that I was going to be all right, and asked for something to eat. Yes, I was going to be all right, but the experience left me changed.

For one thing, I really burned out some brain cells. I would lose my train of thought mid-sentence. And I was left genuinely paranoid.

The overdose kicked me out of the drug experience for good. My friends tried to get me back into taking drugs, but a single inhalation of marijuana sent fear rushing through me. Finally, and most importantly, the experience left me with a tremendous sense of gratitude that I was still alive, and a quiet question— why did I choose life? What was there about life that I clung to it so desperately?

I want to put this into some proper perspective. I have always been and remain, gratefully, a pretty emotionally stable person— rarely getting angry, always considerate of others and well liked. During this experience, I did not have any divine revelations or anything like that. It was simply that my entire framework of life was jolted. At the time of the experience, I can only describe it as absolutely harrowing, but now I look back on it with gratitude. The experience took me off one road and put me onto another that has proved to be much more fulfilling. At the time, I had no idea what that road was going to be, but the process was gently driven by the "why life?" question.

When this experience happened, I was still at Northwestern University. My natural inclination in education was toward mathematics and the sciences. While a freshman at Northwestern, I transferred out of Liberal Arts into Engineering School because it was always a struggle to write, but I could "add like hell". I still consider myself of the "scientific" mode.

As I mentioned, this whole ordeal occurred when I was getting into hatha yoga. In hindsight, this synchronicity of events and influences in my life seems more than coincidental.

I was performing the hatha yoga exercises quite regularly, enjoying them very much. Soon, I was doing them about two hours a day, which inspired an interest in the philosophical aspects of yoga. I bought a book called *How to Know God: Patanjali's Yogic Aphorisms*. At that time, I wasn't into God at all but I was into yoga, and here was a simple book on the philosophy of yoga by an Indian named Swami Prabhavananda.

This book was in dramatic contrast to any type of reading I usually did. "Give me mathematics or give me death" was my motto, but here I was reading a philosophy book, on "Eastern" philosophy no less. Well, that book was remarkable, and it had a profound effect on me. Here was a wonderful life philosophy, more complete than anything I could conceive of myself, or had ever heard of in any Western psychologies. Its words affirmed themselves within me, and I continually found myself nodding "yes". It spoke of an intimate relationship between man and God. This was a different God from the one that I had been taught about in the Jewish faith. This was a God who existed inside me—my own highest self. For whatever reason, this resonated with me. It spoke of the inner life and the role of the spiritual Teacher and how the teacher serves the aspiration of the seeker.

I read about a very special category of spiritual Teacher—the Avatar, the divine incarnation. We in the West are familiar with the Christ as such a Teacher, but here I read the names of Buddha, Krishna and Ramakrishna alongside that of the Christ. Now, having been raised in the Jewish faith, this was all relatively foreign to me for the most part, but it was so compelling that I was convinced of the *possibility* that it was true. The God it defined was a God I could deal with, a God who lived inside me and was my own higher nature. Frankly, this book inspired me tremendously. I still re-read it from time to time.

At Northwestern, I began to change directions as well. I was a senior at the time, and had finished my engineering curricula. I was required to take some courses in the humanities to round out my education, so I took advantage of this to continue my "why life?" investigation. Because I had just read of the Buddha, I decided to take a course in Buddhism, studying the *Dhammapada* with a Buddhist monk. (The *Dhammapada* represents the essential teachings of the Buddha.)

I dabbled in many of the great scriptures. I read the *Ramayana*, the story of Rama, an Indian prince whom Hindus embrace as an Avatar, a man/God, who lived thousands of years before the Christ. I read the *Mahabharata*, which is the life story of Sri Krishna, another God in human form. Many readers may be familiar with the *Bhagavad-Gita*, "The Song Celestial". It is considered one of the greatest Hindu texts and is a discourse between Sri Krishna and his foremost disciple, Arjuna, about the meaning of life and how to approach God. It is often called the "Bible" of India. The *Bhagavad-Gita* is one chapter of the *Mahabharata*. I studied bits and pieces of the *Upanishads* and the *Vedas*, considered the oldest spiritual scriptures on earth.

I read a book called *Ramakrishna and His Disciples*, by Christopher Isherwood, and had a wonderful experience. Ramakrishna was a great spiritual Teacher who lived right at the turn of the

> "Spirituality is not merely tolerance. It is not even acceptance. It is the feeling of universal oneness. Spirituality is not mere hospitality to others' faith in God. It is the absolute recognition and acceptance of their faith in God as one's own. Difficult, but not impossible, for this has been the experience and practice of all spiritual Masters of all times. — S.C.

past century, in the late 1800s. As I would turn the pages, reading certain passages, the sweetest fragrance seemed to come off
the pages, my hair would stand on end and tears would spontaneously well up. I was filled with a great sense of joy. These
experiences came entirely unexpectedly.

And then I took a giant leap for someone raised in the Jewish
faith—I read most of the New Testament. In the Jewish faith,
you just don't believe in the Christ as Christians define him. You
may hear things like, "He was a nice man", or "He was a great
teacher", or even "He really didn't exist". But in no way was he
the Messiah predicted in the Bible. So to read the New Testament
was indeed a giant leap.

Wonderfully, I was greeted with the same experience as
when I read about Ramakrishna. Again, fragrance would rise off
the pages and tears would well up in my eyes. That experience
left me with a profound and intimate link with the Christ as a
Teacher. (Many people have suggested that I was a priest in a
previous lifetime. Reincarnation ... I know, that's a whole other
subject.)

Here it's important to clarify that I was raised not necessarily
"believing" in any one thing. I was not brought up to believe in
any kind of conscious spiritual processing at all, save for that of
being a moral and good human being. My religious rearing as a
Jew was, for the most part, a socio-cultural thing. I would call
myself more "Jew-ish" than Jewish. And certainly, the concept
that there is *only one way* of spiritual processing was completely
foreign to me! Quite the contrary. My Jewish upbringing was such
that I was quite tolerant and open to all sorts of possibilities.

What I witnessed in all this reading was very important. Here
were 10,000 years of recorded spiritual histories that were all
saying basically the same thing. 10,000 years! They may have
said it for a different time and a different culture, but the essence

of what they were all saying was the same. (We will explore what was said in a later chapter.) This was in stark contrast to my scientific training that was constantly in the process of disproving itself. When I began my physics studies at Northwestern, I started studying Newton and his falling apple. Before leaving Northwestern, I was studying Einstein's physics that explains that Newton's physics was a good approximation, but wrong.

This is consistent with the nature of science. Science is always in the process of discounting its previously accepted truths. At one time the earth was the centre of the universe. Now, of course, we know that the earth rotates around the sun. Science is constantly changing its version of the truth. Just recently, I viewed a documentary from the late 1950s on what constituted a good diet—bacon and eggs fried in lots of butter, with white toast smothered in more butter ... mmm. How different the prescribed scientific diet is today! Ironically, no matter what day, year or era it is, science admits, "Well that was then, but *now* we know..."

But here in my readings were 10,000 years of recorded spiritual wisdom and history, and the truths and teachings spoken of remained essentially the same over time. This suggested to me that all these teachers and learned men must have been tapping into the same source. It was enough to convince me to investigate further.

One thing all the teachers addressed was the necessity and role of the Teacher. I mention this here because it is relevant to my own beginnings. I'll leave an in-depth discussion for later, because I feel the reasons why a Teacher seems to be necessary are easier to grasp once one understands more of the picture. But it is relevant to mention it now, because of the role it played in my own experience.

Because every scripture addressed the necessity of a teacher, I was convinced that I should have one. After all, if Ramakrishna,

Here is Sri Chinmoy as you might expect to see an Indian Guru —
wearing the Indian garb. This photo was taken in a casual moment
when he was chatting with some of his students.

the Buddha and the Christ were influenced by spiritual Teachers in their formative years, geez, it didn't take a whole lot of
humility on my part to think I could probably use one.

When I returned to my home in New York from Northwestern,
I started my search for a Teacher. I contacted every yoga organ-
ization in New York City. Upon opening the literature I received
from the various organizations I contacted, I was regularly
greeted by two things: one was what I call the "sage" look—a
smiling, long-haired bearded man. Well, I already had the sage
look myself, so that didn't impress me! The second thing was a
fee, and the fee was a complete turn-off. It just intuitively struck
me as wrong. Look at the great Teachers. When did they ever
charge a fee?

The last place I contacted was a place called "Yoga of Westchester". Now, I have to tell you that, based on the name alone,

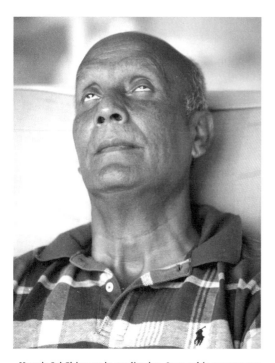

Here is Sri Chinmoy in meditation. It was this appearance that convinced me he knew what meditation is at a very high level. I love this photo because here is an Indian Master in a very high consciousness, wearing a nice Polo shirt. It shows that the inner life can and should go together with the outer life.

this was the last place I ever expected to find a meditation class or teacher. Westchester is definitely upper-middle class, for the most part. I expected to find a group of house-mums who got together, stood on their heads and then had tea! (*Please* forgive my political incorrectness.) When I called, I was greeted by a very nice woman who, upon my inquiry about meditation, informed me that "if you would like to meditate with a genuine master of the highest caliber, Sri Chinmoy is offering a free meditation at Columbia University". Well, *free* was the thing that caught me, and so I went.

If you're expecting some cosmic tale about my experience at this point, you'll be disappointed. I attended that meditation with a friend. It was okay, but I wasn't particularly impressed. I was handed a brochure on Sri Chinmoy and meditation. I sat in the back of a large auditorium. There were all kinds of people there—young, old, nuns, hippies and more. About ten minutes was all that I could take. I left with my friend, bought a bottle of Mateus wine and sipped the evening away in Central Park. So much for the cosmic, spiritual experience!

It turns out that Yoga of Westchester was the closest yoga centre to my home and I decided to take hatha yoga classes there. In my various readings, the "appearance" of someone who was meditating in a high consciousness was described—the eyes half-closed, seemingly looking in and yet looking out. It was at Yoga of Westchester where I saw pictures of Sri Chinmoy in meditation. He *had* that appearance *(see previous page)*. Prior to that, I had never witnessed anyone who fit that description.

There was no question in my mind that he was experiencing some states of consciousness beyond the norm. Based on this simple academic recognition, I decided I would find out what he was about. I was going to give him three months to show me what he knew.

I started by reading his books and meditating as he prescribed. It seemed to work. After a month or so, I decided to formally become a student.

A confirmation of sorts

It was the fall of 1971. In those days, in order to become a student, you had a personal interview with Sri Chinmoy. Guru lived in a simple, modest home in Queens, New York. I arrived there not knowing what to expect. As I approached the front door, Sri Chinmoy was there to greet me. He opened the door, indicating with a gesture from his hand that I should come in.

I didn't know what to do, so again with a gesture he indicated I should sit down, which I did. Somewhat at a loss for the appropriate words (I mean, just what do you say to a supposedly "God-realised Master"?), I said nothing.

He simply requested, "Please look at me," which I did. Sri Chinmoy began to meditate.

Now, when Sri Chinmoy meditates, it is very obvious. His eyes move back and forth rapidly and penetratingly. You can see from his facial expression that he seems to be inwardly climbing and searching. The point is, as he directed that meditative gaze towards me, I was overcome with the distinct feeling that he was looking right through me and, as he did so, that he knew me completely. It was just an impression, but one I couldn't ignore.

His meditation ended and, in the Indian tradition, he bowed to me with folded hands, a bow which I returned. Then he asked quite casually, "Your parents won't mind you doing this?"

I responded "No," somewhat surprised that he would even ask. My parents had experienced four sons' worth of mischief and seemed to handle it all with more than enough aplomb. I couldn't imagine them minding me doing this.

Then he reiterated, "Your mother won't mind?"

I responded with a "correcting" tone. "No, my mother would *never* mind," I said, thinking to myself that perhaps my father might mind, but never my mother. My father was in the process of rediscovering his own Judaic roots, subsequent to his mother's recent passing. He was attending temple quite regularly, so I could anticipate him possibly suggesting that I consider attending temple with him instead. But the thought of my mother minding was inconceivable.

You see, my mother had done most of the rearing of the children. My father was married to his pharmacy, although his loving influence was always present in our home and in my life. My father would always joke that the key to my parents' success in marriage was that my mother recognized her proper place in the family. She would make the minor decisions—such as where we should live, where the kids should go to school, what kind of car we should drive—he explained, but she would "surrender" the truly important decisions to him—decisions such as whether we should send a man to the moon, or what our policy should be with regards to China.

At any rate, my mother had already experienced her two older sons getting into their share of teenage mischief. Jackie, my oldest brother, was straight out of the "American Graffiti" era, and definitely one of the tough guys. Lenny was Fabian reborn in a 1957 Chevy. And I was a full-blown hippie. (My youngest brother, Billy, didn't wait for his teenage years to create problems. He was a monster from birth, but in my opinion, turned out the best of the lot.)

Anyway, let me give you an example of how my mother handled my mischief, to show why I was sure she wouldn't mind my foray into meditation. I was arrested for possession of marijuana (eventually, everybody got arrested in those days), and my mother was summoned to bail me

My dad and mum

out. God bless my mother! She came storming into the Scarsdale Police Station absolutely irate—not at me—at the police! "How can you arrest my son? Why don't you get the real criminals? So what if he smokes a little marijuana ... all the kids do!"

My mother was a short but large woman. When asked her height, she would describe herself as "5 by 5" and it was pretty accurate. And because she was heavy, she was always hot. After bailing me out, she said, quite deliberately in front of the police, "Sandy, next time you get arrested make sure it's an air-conditioned police station, or I'm not coming down to bail you out."

Such was my mother's tolerance and love. So I was definitely correct in assuring Sri Chinmoy that my mother would never mind, or so I thought. I even thought it was somewhat humorous that he would ask.

At home I began to meditate as Sri Chinmoy prescribed. My mother could not help but notice the changes. My hair and beard disappeared. I was getting up earlier. I would close my door whenever I was in my room. The occasional fragrance of incense would waft through the apartment. Furthermore, all my drug-associate friends disappeared from my life. Certainly, these were all positive things for which every mum would be grateful, so you would think.

Then one afternoon, seemingly out of nowhere ... "Sandy, what are you into now?" she inquired.

I explained that I had decided to study meditation and, for three months, I was going to study with an Indian spiritual Master.

You can imagine my shock and dismay when then and there she threatened, "If you are going to do that, I disown you and you'll have to move out of my house."

I couldn't believe my ears. I had never heard words such as these coming from my mother!

"I don't want you becoming a monk!" she screamed.

I had no idea that she would have any concept of what this whole thing was about in the first place! "I don't want to become a monk either!" I reassured, and tried to convince her that this was just going to be for a few months. It was not enough. There was no appeasing her. She "disowned" me so completely that indeed I had to move out of the house! Eventually, she accepted me back when she saw that things were okay—I wasn't renouncing the world, although that acceptance, frankly, was never complete on her part.

This experience confirmed for me that my immediate impression in that brief initial moment of meditation was correct. Sri Chinmoy had seen something in my life that in my wildest dreams I had not anticipated. As it turned out, I was completely wrong about both my parents' responses, because my father became very receptive to the whole idea. In fact, focused around my meditative life, my father and I rediscovered a close-ness which we had lost during my hippie era, a closeness that I shall always cherish.

He once confessed, "I'm very grateful to Guru for the impact that he's had on your life."

During my hippie phase, my father and I experienced an irreconcilable and very painful generation gap. I was my dad's favorite son and my hippie-drug life was a source of tremendous disappointment to my father. But, as a result of the influence of Sri Chinmoy in my life and the changes that came with that, my father and I became closer than we'd ever been. As I am writing this, I'm remembering him. Allow me to confess that tears of gratitude are welling up in my eyes for his love.

I officially began this journey in early 1971. I began it having read much and thinking I knew a lot. Now, some 40-plus years later, I *know* that I know next to nothing, but at least I am confi-dent in that little knowledge!

Just What Did Those Teachers Say?

I suspect that many of you may be familiar with some of the books and teachings I mentioned in the previous chapter. Recall that I read them as part of my own introduction to the spiritual life. Allow me to ask this question:

Would you agree that what those books say, in essence, is that, in some way, shape or form, you have a spiritual aspect and you've got to deal with it?

Would you say, "yes" or "no"? Inevitably, when I ask this question, nine out of ten people raise their hands in agreement. The others don't, because they assume the question is rhetorical and the answer is obviously affirmative.

Forgive me, this is a little bit of a trick question because this is not what the books and teachings say. It's close, but not spot on. What they say is not that you merely *have* a spiritual nature, but that you *are* that spiritual nature.

In fact, they say that the very purpose of our human existence is to rediscover that inner reality, to grow into it and ultimately become a perfect expression of it. In religious terminology, life's purpose is to become one with God and become a perfect instrument for the will of God. This is that mystical union referred to as God-realisation or Self-realisation.

> The aim of life is to become conscious of the Supreme Reality.
>
> S.C.

Furthermore, these great Teachers would add that the casualness with which we relate to our spiritual nature is the source of all of our struggles in life.

Most of us are comfortable with the possibility that human life has some spiritual dimension. But it is a very rare human being who seeks to place that spiritual dimension first and foremost in his/her life.

Consider the difference between saying "I am the body, with a spiritual nature," and "I am that spiritual nature meant to express itself through this body." This is a small change in words, but it has a large impact in how we approach life.

If our primary identity is, first and foremost, the body, then immediately we are limited. We are limited because the physical itself is limited. We relate to our spiritual nature casually, or we may even ignore it completely. Hence, the great teachers refer to "ignorance", not in the sense of stupidity, but as the act of ignoring our spiritual aspect or development*.

However, implicit in a spiritual identification is a sense of "unlimitedness". In fact, all the great Teachers have suggested that we have limitless capacity to know love, to create peace

---

* *The Yogic concept that man is inherently divine is in stark contrast to the Western Christian concept that man is by nature a sinner. I don't actually see this in the Christ's teachings. "Sin" is the consequence of ignorance. However, when ignorance is illumined, sin disappears.*

inwardly, to be creative and serve outwardly. This affirmation is based on their direct experience of their own spiritual natures.

Why is this dis-identification with our spiritual natures at the root of much of our life struggles and stresses? Let's examine.

There are two questions which constantly haunt us as human beings. We deal with these questions every day of our lives: "Who am I?" and "Why am I here?" Now, I am not suggesting that you wake up in the morning and ask, "Gee, who am I and why am I here?" I am suggesting that we live our lives in such a fashion that these questions are in some way addressed.

Consider how you introduce and define yourself. You have a name and a place where you live. You have an occupation which (hopefully) suits you. You earn some income to suit your comfort level. You choose a style of clothing which is "uniquely you". You go to school to "become something". Examine these definitions. None of these things really describes who you are, but rather what you do and where you do it!

We all feel the need to affirm our existence somehow. We all seek to carve out some space about which we can say, "This is me." This need operates subtly in our day-to-day actions. I witness it in my classes all the time. The first person comes in. First, they may not be sure they are in the right place because no one else is there. They come in and sit down,

> Be ye therefore perfect, even as your Father which is in heaven is perfect.
>
> THE CHRIST

usually in the back left corner. With each new person entering, the room becomes carved up into nice equal pieces (unless the people know each other). Person two will sit in the front right (rarely in the front row!). Person three will sit somewhere in the middle, and so on. Ah, to witness the strain on the person who enters and must be the first to sit in a seat between two people!

Imagine you are alone in a lecture room which seats 500 people. A second person comes in and sits right next to you! Most people would feel terribly uncomfortable, and wonder if they are sitting next to some recently escaped psychopath, and perhaps find some convenient excuse to leave (or enter into a nice quiet prayer that the room would fill up quickly!).

> He is born to no purpose, who, having had the rare privilege of being born human, does not realise God in this life.
>
> ᔆ SRI RAMAKRISHNA

Consciously or unconsciously, we are all playing the self-affirmation game—and most often we affirm ourselves first as a body with very little conscious awareness of our spiritual lives. "I've got to earn a certain income." "I want to live in this or that town." "I want to be an architect, a computer scientist, a chiropractor." "I love chocolate ice cream." This is what makes me "me".

When our self-affirmation is based on the outer nature, then we have no choice but to be conditioned by our outer surroundings. We are "advertised" into buying things, we are socialised into behaviour patterns, we are "parent-ised" to grow up into a particular profession. (My father always wanted me to become a doctor. It is a little-known universal law that every Jewish pharmacist wants at least one son to become a doctor.) To a large extent, this conditioning makes us victims of our outer circumstances. Very often we'll find ourselves doing things not because we know them to be right "from within", but because it is expected of us "from without". For example, as a youngster I used to preach and preach to my parents to stop smoking. But then I lit up in front of them at the ripe old age of 16. Why? Because all my friends were smoking. This was my right of passage into adulthood. So, despite what I knew to be right, I allowed my outer circumstances to influence me to make a wrong life choice.

Allow me to suggest that the degree to which we affirm our exist-ence, first and foremost, in things external to us, things that are physical, things that are bodily oriented first, is the degree to which we lose touch with who we truly are.

Let me make it even more emphatic! **You can never, never affirm your existence in terms of things that are external to you.** It's impossible. It's built into the life game. You cannot do it.

Why is this the case? The answer is simple, although not necessarily obvious. What is there about your surroundings that prevents you from affirming yourself in relationship to it? What one dynamic operates in *everything external*—in the walls, the trees, the occupations, even our own bodies? (Now, think about this before you read the answer. Remember, this is supposed to be a self-study. And to be sure you don't just peek at the next sentence, I'm putting in a blank space below to give you time to think...)

● ● ●

(Are you thinking?)

The answer? Change. Yes, change is the only thing present in everything external. Everything in the outer world is in a state of flux. Nothing is permanent, not even our own body. And therefore, if our self-affirmation is built upon things external to us, *our self-affirmation must be impermanent as well.*

As a consequence, it's natural then that we play our various self-affirmation games with more intensity. Ubiquitous in human kind is a process of "upward mobility". This upward mobility operates at all levels of humanity everywhere. The homeless person on the street wants another quarter so he can buy coffee or something like that. The president of a major corporation seeks to acquire another company. We try to have more possessions, more wealth, more fame, more power—all in an attempt to claim more of the world, to make our sense of self more permanent. Ultimately, it all fails us.

Ironically, the more we attempt to cling to the world in hopes of self-affirmation, the more it seems to slip through our fingers. Upon reflection, we may be left feeling, "Is that all there is?" Ultimately, with the recognition of this futile effort, we reach a point that in spiritual literature is referred to as "divine discontent". It is referred to as "discontent" because this point is often arrived at after crisis, frustration or stress. It is called "divine" because this same point is often the dawn of a most remarkable inner journey. Divine discontent—the recognition that the thing you've been most intimate with all your life is the thing you are least familiar with. That thing is yourself!

How often we will intuitively say that happiness lies within, but how rarely do we look there! Instead, we try to script ourselves into some activity to make us happy, or we try to preoccupy ourselves by filling our time with pleasure. We have difficulty sitting in a room alone with nothing to do. We find silence painfully awkward.

How many times we say, "If I could only find out what to do, then I would be happy." That is just the opposite of what the great Teachers say we should do, which is to be happy within, and then bring that happiness outward into every action we do. *Happiness is a state of being, not doing.* Our inner happiness frees us to do whatever is necessary in our outer lives.

Our inner environment is the one thing we carry with us into every encounter. If we can create an inner environment of happiness, poise, dignity, peace and love, then we can carry those qualities into every action, every job, every relationship. Again, our inner environment is the only thing over which we can claim rightful responsibility.

Recognize this, and recognize this now. If you want the world to be more loving and peaceful, *then your first obligation must be to make yourself more loving and peaceful.* Then, and only then, are you in a position to offer these qualities to the world.

> **"**What is meant by spiritual perfection?
> It is the constant capacity
> to live in God and to reveal Him
> in one's every movement.
> — s.c.

The nature of the mind

At this point we might ask the question, "What is there about our inner constitution that allows us to get so lost? If we are essentially spiritual, infinite, unlimited, then why do we fail to immediately see it or feel it?"

Exercise / Observing the mind

Let's see if we can find out a little something about the nature of our minds. In this exercise, you are going to use the mind as an observer of its own workings—you will watch it do its thing. This is not a meditation exercise, so the ABCs we spoke of are not important.

For this exercise, please return to the lighted candle. Simply begin by looking at the candle. Don't concentrate on it, just look at it. Use the candle as a reference point to watch the movements and thoughts of your mind. The candle is to simply serve as a starting point from which you should watch the currents of your thoughts. Sit comfortably in a chair and take three to five minutes to simply observe your own mental movements. Observe how you think. Where does the mind go—how does it behave?

Well, where did your mind go? What did it do? If your mind is like most people's, it begins a river of rambling. It spontaneously responds to stimuli by projecting thoughts forward. For example, a bus will go by and as the bus passes, your mind moves along with it. You may notice it being loud, wonder where it is heading, and from there you may think of where you have to go later that day.

Not only does it simply respond to stimuli, but the mind will seek out fresh stimuli. For example, imagine in a classroom that someone new walks in while the class is in progress. Typically, heads turn to see who it is, as if everyone is expecting someone. Then the mind kicks in with its evaluation-criticism process, for example: "I like their clothes," or "How dare they come in so late," or "Gee, they could at least be quiet coming in so late."

Often the rambling is of the free association type. For example, your thoughts may go from the candle flame to the kitchen stove to what you're going to have for dinner tonight to the fact that you forgot to make reservations for dinner at the restaurant. And of course, as the mind travels, it calls upon an emotional pool to add feelings to the thoughts. For example, you may get upset with yourself because you forgot to make reservations.

> "The mind has endless questions. The heart has only one question: "Am I really pleasing my Lord Supreme in His own Way?" — S.C.

I recall one extreme instance in a class when I had to stop this simple exercise after a minute or so because a woman in the front row started having an anxiety attack. When I inquired about her experience, she explained her anxiety this way, "My God, am I going to have to do this at home in front of my three kids? They'll think I've gone over the edge!"

Another of the mind's favorite activities is list making/agenda creating. It is our inner "Day-Timer". Again, it may borrow from our emotional pool to add drama. If the list is something we look forward to, it calls on enthusiasm. "Oh boy, tomorrow I'm going to Disneyland." If the list is long or dreaded, the mind calls on one of its best friends, worry. "Oh my God, I've got so much to do that I'll never make it."

It's not unusual that the "enthusiasm-worry train" carries us forward and backward in time. We might be having a wisdom tooth extracted in three weeks, but we worry about it now, and in so doing, we destroy the opportunity that the present moment offers to experience joy. Or, frequently we'll feel guilty about something that happened years ago, again destroying the present moment's opportunity to experience joy.

Consider this. When was the last time you witnessed your mind sitting still and satisfied in the present moment? Or in silence? Most of us are so estranged from silence that we find it uncomfortable and awkward. In an extreme case, some people confess that their minds "scream" at them. They seek meditation with the hope it will help them escape from their noise-mind shackles.

In the course of its wanderings, the mind does not always "stick to the facts". Beyond thinking of past/future events, it can fantasise about possibilities, creating its own truth as it goes along! One of my favorite examples of this is an experience of Mark, a friend of mine. (I'm only giving his first name to protect the innocent!)

> " My silence bridges the gulf between my life's success and my life's failure. My silence does not magnify my defects. Nor does it connive at them. My silence transforms my defects into strength indomitable. ⚘ s.c.

Mark is a big fellow, with an admitted tendency toward ill temper. Every evening *after* driving home from work, it was his habit to walk to the local grocery store, pick up his next day's food and walk back home. This is how he would chill out from the day's work and get in a little exercise to boot.

One particular evening he had worked quite late, so he drove directly to the grocery store on his way home from work. *But* when he left the grocery, forgetting that he had driven there directly from work, as was his habit, he walked home!

Well, you might guess what happened. The next day, he was about to leave for work when he discovered, of course, that his car was missing. But not just missing—it was stolen! He called the police and reported it so, and then arranged for a ride to work. Well, Mark was really upset about this (as we all might be) and while obsessing about it during the day, he figured out who must have stolen the car. He *knew* it was the problem kids on the block. Now his temper started kicking in and he planned his confrontation and how he was going to get his car back.

That evening, after getting a ride home from work, he embarked on his usual walk to the grocery store. The startling truth was revealed when he saw his car in the parking lot! Reality set in. He now recalled everything as it actually took place. Now, here is what's really interesting about this saga. Mark told me that he couldn't just turn off his anger. He confessed that his mind replayed the theft and his retribution over and over for three days!

The mind is very good at creating its own reality. How many times our mind-life drama convinces us "How tough life is". I recall another dear friend doing precisely this while he and I were sipping a cappuccino at Starbucks—in Singapore! (Yes, Starbucks is in Singapore.) Here we were, escaping miserable winters in a beautiful tropical land, sipping cappuccinos at Starbucks. It's sunny out, beautiful flowers decorate the roadway, and he's "spieling" about how miserable his life was! I reminded him to look around. "This is not misery," I said. Then I went on to list any number of countries currently experiencing famine and war. "That's misery," I said. He smiled at the acknowledgment of his own mental disease.

Finally, let's not forget one of the mind's favorite activities— analyzing: "Let's see, the candle flame is one inch high, yellow with a blue centre, on a candlestick that's six inches tall, etc., etc." One of the interesting things about the mind's analytical process is that in the course of analyzing, it separates and tries to break things down into small parts.

Think of a flower. How does the mind identify or know a flower? The very nature of a flower is to offer beauty and to offer that beauty selflessly. It does not ask to be looked at. But how does the mind see the flower? "The lily ... is pink with eight petals outside and twelve stamen inside." Want to know it better? Slice into it and see how its stem is made. This is the mind of my "scientific orientation". It has its value, certainly. But in fact to know something, the mind's tendency is to break it into its smallest parts, categorising and compartmentalising along the way. *The mind separates.*

> I must immensely enjoy
> My heart's millions of pluses
> And vehemently reject
> My life's hundreds of minuses.
>
> — s.c.

I believe a major reason why we are often lost to the underlying oneness of all things has to do with the degree to which we have allowed the mind—the analytical, rambling, criticising, separating mind—to dominate our life's interactions. Now, let me emphasise that I am *not* suggesting that the mind is evil. Nor am I suggesting that the mind must be excised or ignored. No. But what I am suggesting is that we must modify the behaviour of the mind by developing another part of our inner family—the heart, that is, the spiritual heart.

The great Teachers have suggested that we are, by nature, spiritual, infinite. But, how much of our mind's time is spent dwelling in this truth? Instead, the mind is caught in the sensory experiences of the world. As long as we allow the mind to roam freely here and there and consider the mind to be the senior member of our "inner" family, we too will be caught by the world. If you suspect that the meditation process requires some disciplining of the mind, you are correct. Ultimately, meditation will affect all parts of the being, but of particular importance is the retraining of the mind to see with the eyes of the heart. In fact, you might note that *concentration* is an important first step in learning to meditate. We'll explore concentration techniques in a little bit.

◉ An interesting side note

Often at the end of a year, Sri Chinmoy would give his students a meditative exercise to practise for the coming year. For example, in 1991 he asked his students to not be critical of anybody. He asked, "What value is your criticism of other people? Your energy can be better spent on your own self-perfection instead of criticising others."

There was an additional instruction. He asked that in our morning meditation we do two things. First, we should think of seven of our own imperfections and simply offer them like flowers to God. Secondly, think of three of our good qualities and offer these like flowers to God as well. Then, he affirmed, we would see that our imperfections would diminish while our perfections would increase.

Later that year at a gathering of 100 or so of my fellow students, I had an interesting experience. I polled people and discovered that for the most part we had a common dilemma. To come up with seven imperfections was no problem. But to come up with three good qualities was tough. We might be able to say, "I am a pretty good person, basically." But to come up with our good qualities was difficult.

> "It is enthusiasm and not criticism that can perfect us. Self-criticism is not the correct way. What we constantly need is an inner cry. It is through self-search and self-illumination that we can arrive at perfection. What we need at every moment is enthusiasm in measureless measure and not criticism by others or even self-criticism. ✑ s.c.

Now, examine how you view yourself, or perhaps more appropriately, consider how you *think* of yourself. Are you more familiar with your weaknesses than your strengths? When you are confronted with a new task, which comes first, doubt or confidence? Can you identify what makes you good? Well, start the process right now of changing the way you think about yourself and others.

Exercise / Curb your criticism

Take a day to not be critical of others or yourself. Choose one day of the week for this, for example, no-criticism Tuesdays. You'll be shocked at how much free time is left in your mind! You'll be equally amazed at how much happier you are.

You may be one of those who are frustrated with your mind's noise. Don't fret. Just as a lethargic, out-of-shape body can be made fit with proper diet and appropriate exercise, so can a restless, undisciplined mind be made fit—tuned into a controlled and useful instrument, with a proper diet of correct thought and regular exercise of concentration and other spiritual disciplines.

You'll read the word "consciousness" on many of these pages. It is a concept which is central to any discussion on meditation. What does consciousness mean? Typically, responses run from "awareness" to "perception" to "values" to "inner knowledge", and these are all good answers. In one particular class, one person said that it's "being aware", while another person suggested it's the "awareness of being". Should you put these two responses together,

Consciousness

you'll come close to what consciousness is: *being aware with the awareness of your being.*

Consciousness is a link between our inner awareness and our outer awareness. When you say, "I'm conscious of something," it's more than mere outer awareness. Instead, it represents an awareness in the deeper part of your being. When offering a class in a school setting, I may be aware that there are people in other areas of the school, but

I am much more conscious of those individuals in the class. Sri Chinmoy defines consciousness in a very specific way:

> "Consciousness is the inner spark or inner link in us, the golden link within us that connects our highest and most illumined part with our lowest and most unillumined part."

"Human consciousness is made up primarily of limitation, imperfection, bondage and ignorance. This consciousness wants to remain on earth. It gets joy in the finite: in family, in society, in earthly affairs. Divine consciousness is made up of Peace, Bliss, Divine Power and so forth. Its nature is to expand constantly. Human consciousness feels that there is nothing more important than earthly pleasure. Divine consciousness feels that there is nothing more important and significant than heavenly Joy and Bliss on earth. Human consciousness tries to convince us that we are nowhere near the Truth or fulfilment. It tries to make us feel that God is somewhere else, millions of miles away from us. But Divine consciousness makes us feel that God is right here, inside each life-breath, inside each heartbeat, inside everyone and everything around us."

(The Summits of God-Life: Samadhi and Siddhi)

Our love of the Consciousness-Light can and will expedite our achievement in the body. ⚘ s.c.

Sri Chinmoy adds that once you experience consciousness, it immediately suggests that you have some spiritual source. Imagine that your eyes are closed and that a fresh rose is placed right in front of your nose. You catch the fragrance of the rose and *know* that a rose is before you. The fragrance suggests the source, in this case, the flower. This phenomenon is quite familiar. We've all probably had the experience of catching a sweet fragrance while walking or jogging, and we usually turn to see the source from which the sweetness emanates. The fragrance suggests its source, the flower.

Think of consciousness as the fragrance of your inner flower, the spiritual self. This spiritual self may be called by different names. Some call it "self", or "spirit". The Hindu would refer to it as the "*Atman*", while the Westerner might say "individual consciousness" or "soul". It matters not what word you use, as long as you appreciate the concept. For our discussion, I'll use the term "soul".

> "Our devotion to the Consciousness-Light can and will expedite our achievement in the vital. s.c.

So, consciousness is the fragrance of the soul. When you get a taste of consciousness, you know that the soul-flower exists. In fact, the relationship of consciousness to the soul is more intimate than the relationship of a flower to its fragrance. You can separate the flower from its fragrance, but you cannot separate consciousness from the soul. They are, in fact, the same substance but in different form.

To understand this better, let me use a different analogy. Instead of a flower, consider the soul as a snowball. Consciousness, then, is water emanating from the snowball. Like water and snow, consciousness and the soul are the same substance but in slightly different forms. Now, let's extend this metaphor one step further.

If the soul is the snowball and water is our human consciousness, then perhaps there is an all-pervading "vapor". This vapor would represent a universal consciousness. This is precisely the religion-spiritual life model: There exists an all-pervading vapor—a universal consciousness, or God, of which my individual consciousness is a part. Using pure religious terminology, God is all-pervading and omnipresent, and the soul is part and parcel of God's existence and of the same substance as God.

Now, let's explore how this relates to our self-affirmation game. A little soul (snowball) lands someplace, say New York, and it goes through its life experience. In the course of its life experience, it rolls through the grass and over a few Coke tabs, picking them up as it rolls along. Of course, at the same time, other snowball-souls are landing in different places and are going through their own life experiences. Inevitably, the New York snowball meets and greets another snowball, one from California. The Californian is covered with mud and tabs from 7-Up.

> Our surrender to the Consciousness-Light can and will expedite our achievement in the mind.
>
> S.C.

The affirmation process begins. (I'll play the role of the New Yorker). "Well, I'm brought up in a different place than the Californian, I have a different colour, and I prefer Coke to 7-Up." I see how I am alike and different from the Californian and all those I encounter in an attempt to affirm myself.

"Aha! Now I know what makes me 'me'," I declare. I identify myself with my accumulated shell and, in so doing, I may even *ignore* my snowball core completely.

This is the body/physical, self-affirmation process. That person is a woman and I'm a man; she has long hair; we both have brown-coloured hair. Here's another man. He's Asian, he's African, he's got gray hair and I've got brown hair. She's a medical doctor, while I'm a chiropractor. And admittedly, to a certain extent, I succeed in affirming my existence by comparing and seeing how different and how similar I am from this person and that person.

This is the common method of self-affirmation. But in an inner sense, this method of self-affirmation costs us dearly. In fact, *it's very, very expensive.* Look carefully. In the course of affirming my existence in terms of my externalities, what have I done with regard to my relationships with those around me? (Now think about this before you answer. To make sure you do, I have put in another page break!)

• • •

(Thinking...)

What have I done? I have separated myself from them. While it's true that I have affirmed my existence, in the course of doing so, I've separated myself from the rest of the world. Now, why is this so costly?

Remember when I posed the question as to whether peace and love were important in your life? Did you agree? Look at these qualities. (This is another very important question.) Are these qualities based on separation or oneness? Oneness, of course.

If the primary way in which we affirm ourselves separates us from others, this flies in the face of our ability to know real love or real peace. We cannot do it. This is what makes it is so costly.

There must be some other way to affirm our existence without separation. Fortunately, there is another way, and with it, one more analogy.

Consider a wave in the ocean. The wave is a wonderful metaphor for human life. It has a beginning (birth) and it has an end (death). The wave starts small, swells and then shrinks again, ultimately returning its content to its source, the ocean. In human life, we go through a similar process. We are born of essential elements, grow, and finally, upon death, these essential elements are returned. Each wave has a direction and a size. We could, should we choose, give a name to each wave. There's more.

> Our constant and inseparable oneness with the Consciousness-Light can and will expedite our achievement in the heart. — S.C.

If we had the power to instantaneously stop each wave and examine it from moment to moment, it would appear to change very little, but we know over the course of time how much it changes. Doesn't human life present itself that way? Each day we wake up and we appear constant, yet over the course of time, how much we change. In reality, the wave is constantly being influenced by the waters to either side of it and beneath it. We, as humans, are constantly being influenced and reshaped by our surroundings. Indeed, our lives are very much like the wave.

If we declare ourselves to be merely the body and all its physical associations, then we're saying, "I am the wave." In the extreme case, we ignore our relationship to the ocean completely.

Now, instead of saying, "I am the wave," imagine yourself going underneath the surface just a few inches. Dive under your surface, under the water a few inches. How do you view yourself then? What are you? Are you just the wave? No! Immediately you see yourself as part of the larger ocean. You see yourself as the water from which all waves are created. You might look up and say, "Aha! That's my wave! That's the place where I'm to express myself ... that's where I'm interacting outwardly." But from beneath the surface of the water, you clearly see that what you truly are is the water from which all waves are created.

> **My** Lord's Fulfilment-Ocean
> Is eagerly waiting for the arrival
> Of my life's enthusiasm-river.
>
> s.c.

Placing yourself under the water only a few inches radically changes your reality. In exactly the same way, when you meditate, when you turn inward and dive beneath your surface consciousness just a little, your perspective of yourself changes equally radically. You see yourself not merely as the body, but as this inner substance—this water—this consciousness from which all beings are formed. You get a glimpse that your reality-consciousness is part and parcel of an ocean of consciousness and all of its waves. *It is this experience that creates the foundation of oneness upon which the seeds of true love can now be sown.*

Let's continue with our wave-ocean exploration. Imagine now that you go to the bottom of the ocean. You are the ocean itself. *Is it not clear that each and every wave is an extension of the ocean's reality-existence?* This is the experience of the great Teachers—everything that we experience, even our individual selves, is in fact an expression of the God-ocean or universal consciousness.

Finally, when our consciousness is completely merged with the ocean, this is the Nirvana, the Realisation, of which the great Teachers speak. In reality, we are the ocean of consciousness itself and our individual lives are nothing other than the infinite ocean expressing itself in infinitely many finite wave forms. We have every right to declare, "I am the Ocean." "I and my Father are one." "I am That." "I am He."

These are all utterances that great spiritual Teachers have spoken. And, as was mentioned earlier, every spiritual Teacher has said that this realisation is the very purpose to which we are born. We all have the right to realise this truth for ourselves.

This glorious journey begins with the simple affirmation, "I am spiritual. I'm not merely the body; I am the soul." You may not be sure, but with this humble beginning you are taking your first step toward your true identity.

Breathing and consciousness

There is an entire school of meditation study based on the relationship of breath, and the energy we derive from breath, to consciousness. This study is called *Pranayama*. If you've taken a hatha yoga class, you may have been introduced to certain breath techniques such as alternate nostril breathing, or *kapalabati* (the fire breath).

Sri Chinmoy recommends a breath technique which he calls "the Lion's Breath". I'll introduce you to this now.

Exercise / **The lion's breath**

Remember always to begin with your ABCs. Sit comfortably erect (at your meditation space which you have now set). With the eyes gently closed, make the inner commitment that this next ten, fifteen or twenty minutes is dedicated to your inner life. Nothing else is important for this time.

Allow yourself to feel in the inmost recesses of your heart a sincere inner hunger—for peace, for light, for God, or for whatever spiritual quality appeals to you most. Dwell in that for a minute or two.

I always recommend that you place your hands over your heart. As I mentioned, this will help you to focus on the heart. If you become tired, you can rest your hands on your lap from time to time.

As opposed to quieting the mind with a specific technique, instead we'll ask the mind to concentrate on only one thing. This in itself is a quieting process. Concentrate on the inhaling breath. Imagine that there is a door, window or opening in the centre of your chest, and you are inhaling directly into your spiritual heart. As your inhaling breath flows into the heart, you can almost sense your heart expanding gently with each inhalation. For a minute or two, simply concentrate this way on the inhalation—inhaling directly into your heart.

After a few minutes, in a similar manner, imagine a window or opening at the very crown of your head. As you exhale, imagine the breath exiting the crown of the head and let the breath simply float upwards into the sky. In this way, concentrate on the exhalation for a minute or two.

Now, make the cycle complete: inhale into the heart, exhale out of the crown of the head. Again, do this for a minute or two.

• • •

● ● ●

Now, with each inhalation, feel that you are not merely inhaling air, but instead feel that you are inhaling peace—sweetest peace, abiding peace. Let this peace wash away all anxiety and restlessness and exhale those qualities out of the crown of your head. Inhale peace, exhale restlessness.

After a few minutes, simply concentrate on the inhalation of peace. Let peace fill every aspect of your being.

Now, inhale joy, or happiness, or delight. Feel a sweet and soulful, childlike smile in your heart. Exhale sadness, regret and any other negative qualities. Again, after a few minutes, just concentrate on the inhalation of joy.

Use the same technique with inhaling love and exhaling anger and anything unforgiven.

I always like to end this exercise with a slight variation. Instead of inhaling a quality and bringing it into you, imagine that with each inhalation you are inhaling a sense of "selflessness". Keep nothing for yourself, no desire, no possession—nothing. Let yourself "expand" into "desireless-ness". You can recall your heart's peace, delight and love, and let these qualities expand away from you as well. Expand into a limitless, selfless ocean of peace, joy and love.

One experiences consciousness by loving the Real in himself, by loving the Divine in himself, by crying for the Divine in himself and by constantly giving to Divinity his own reality, which is an inner cry. s.c.

Exercise / **Bringing appropriate closure to your meditation**

Sri Chinmoy recommended that meditation be closed with a minute of gratitude. Regardless of the quality of your meditation, it will help to feel gratitude. Sometimes you eat delicious food, but sometimes you eat yesterday's leftovers! But simply for having the opportunity to eat, we should feel gratitude. Dedicate a minute of your meditation to feeling a sense of gratitude in your heart.

Formally close your meditation by chanting "Shanti" three times soulfully and prayerfully. Chant it slowly, feeling that it comes from your heart.

It should be obvious that you can use the Lion's Breath as an inner "cleanse". You can use any inner pairing—courage-fear, patience-impatience—based on your own inner disposition. In time, you will feel guidance from your own inner being as to how to vary a technique or meditate. Feel the freedom to follow that voice.

I recognize that while describing consciousness in the previous chapter, the references I made may be hard to grasp and that the religious references may or may not appeal to you. You may not care if you realise God—you simply want a little peace of mind. Let me assure you, that is a fine place to begin and a totally legitimate reason to meditate. But please realise that a spiritual process has no meaning to anybody *unless there is some impact, practical impact, in our day-to-day lives*, as indeed there is. You see, consciousness plays out in our lives with a particular set of practical feelings. You'll discover that what we often refer to as a bad day is, in fact, simply a bad consciousness!

To understand this, think of consciousness as a continuum much like a spectrum of light. In the light spectrum, there are ranges of light above

The Consciousness Play

(ultraviolet light) and below (infrared light) the visible spectrum. We can't see these ranges, but science has proven their existence. Now, although we can't see this light, we do experience it. Indeed, an entire cosmetic industry has developed to protect us from the ill-effects of ultraviolet light!

from finite　　　　　　　　　　　　　　　　**to Infinite**

The consciousness continuum

Well, in exactly the same way, there are ranges of consciousness above and below that which we normally experience. Most of humanity lives within a range of what would be the equivalent of "visible" consciousness, but there are ranges of consciousness above and below that which we normally experience.

To get a sense of this continuum, let's identify the extremes. Borrowing from the wave-ocean metaphor we discussed in the last chapter, on one end of the continuum, we are wave-oriented while on the other end of the continuum we are ocean-oriented. Let's examine these extremes more carefully.

When we are wave-oriented, our affirmation comes by virtue of creating a *separate* identity. Our satisfaction comes from grabbing onto the world and declaring it to be ours. Selfishness (I prefer the term "self-full-ness") dominates the personality. "What's in it for me?" becomes the criteria by which we make a decision. I call this the *desire* side of the spectrum.

On the other end of the consciousness spectrum, on the "ocean" side of our range, our affirmation comes by affirming our *oneness*. Our sense of satisfaction comes by virtue of extending ourselves into the world, serving the world. Self-lessness dominates the personality. I refer to this side as the *aspiration* side of the spectrum.

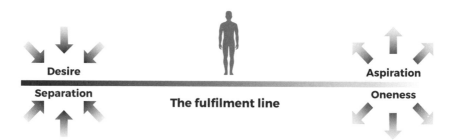

It's important to remember that we all have our own particular range and that both of these sides operate in us. We have our own high side and low side. It is not that one side is bad and the other side good any more than we might say that infrared is bad and ultraviolet good. These realms of consciousness are there for us to experience (and perhaps learn from). Ultimately, where we find ourselves is where we derive the most life-satisfaction, according to our inner evolution.

You may recall that I said that consciousness is a continuum, suggesting we can be painfully wave-like or infinitely ocean-oriented. History has given us some individuals who are so wave-oriented, so selfish, that they are willing to sacrifice the world on their own behalf—the Hitlers and Pol Pots of the world. Fortunately, history has also presented a number of individuals who are so ocean-oriented, so selfless, that they are willing to sacrifice themselves on behalf of the world—the Christ, the Buddha and Sri Krishna, to name a few. I consider Sri Chinmoy among this group.

But our own range lies somewhere in the middle. Of course, we all experience unusually intense wave days when we feel a little disassociated. On those days, the smallest negative intrusion pushes us over the edge. Fortunately we'll also get a glimpse of special ocean days when everything is joyful, regardless of what comes to us.

It's valuable to understand that these ranges of consciousness play out in our lives with their own subset of feelings, emotions and experiences. For example, consider what experiences come to you when you are feeling most separate. What do you feel? (This is another "think about it" before you read on question.)

Here are answers that typically come up in our classes: fear, anger, jealousy, depression, sadness, isolation, feeling unloved, without purpose, prideful, arrogant, insecure and critical. The list becomes gruesome pretty quickly, doesn't it? In the current vernacular, we might say that we are feeling pretty "dysfunctional".

Observe that all these feelings have some degree of inferiority/ superiority issues associated with them, as they should. Separateness mandates that something is bigger/smaller, better/worse, lighter/darker, etc. (It's interesting to note that some people like this realm. It creates drama in their lives. As I said, it's up to the individual where they find satisfaction.)

Now, let's look at the other side of the spectrum, the oneness side. What feelings and experiences do you associate with this side of the spectrum? Love, peace, joy, oneness, purpose, compassion, sense of purpose, enthusiasm. Recognize this list? It looks remarkably similar to the list of qualities that we created when we asked ourselves what would give our life meaning! When we paused to consider what gives our lives meaning, it is now clear—we seek the ocean-consciousness.

I refer to this consciousness continuum as the "fulfilment line". Using this model, now you can see that what we often refer to as a bad day—when we experience disharmony, anger, and all those other qualities that make us uncomfortable with our lives—is not really a bad day at all. It's simply a bad placement on the consciousness continuum.

You can also see that it would be nice if we had some tool by which we can change our range, or shift our range toward the ocean side of the spectrum. We do have such a tool. That tool is meditation. In fact, meditation means "expansion in consciousness". Anything that expands our consciousness is meditation. It can be a beautiful piece of music, the sweet smile of a child, a walk through the forest or a glance up to the sky. On the other hand, none of these things are necessary because you carry within you the most powerful meditative vehicle. Meditation is certainly that quiet time when you dive within and experience your own spiritual heart.

> **"**O voyager of time,
> Onward you proceed
> And offer to the world
> Your achievement-light.
> Much have you to discover,
> Much have you to offer,
> O voyager of time.
>
> S.C.

Herein lies the most exciting part about being born a human being and what separates humanity from the rest of the animal kingdom. First, we have the opportunity to be conscious of our consciousness. And secondly, we have the remarkable opportunity to *consciously change our consciousness!* Yes, we can change! We can examine ourselves and say, "This is good. Let me cultivate it." Or, "This is a weakness. Let me transform it into something better." You carry this capacity wherever you go, whatever you are doing, whenever you are doing. It presents the possibility of a full-time inner occupation.

Our outer occupation changes throughout the day. For example, we wake up in the morning and might spend time with family. That is one script. Then, off to work we go where we follow a different script. After work, we might attend a class or go to the gym, yet another script. And on and on it goes. But, we carry our inner occupation with us wherever we go.

The inner occupation then is to continually experience a shift toward the oneness side of the consciousness continuum. Every day, every hour, every minute, every moment—let us progress towards the ocean side. Every day, every hour, every minute, every moment—let us expand in consciousness. Every day, every hour, every minute, every moment—let us grow in love, in peace, in compassion, nay, in all those qualities which give our lives meaning. This is the opportunity that life itself offers, and I invite you to consider the possibility of making your life sacred.

This process by which we grow in consciousness offers the opportunity to experience ourselves anew each day. Every moment we can be "born anew" by continuing down the consciousness line. When we feel ourselves change, when we witness ourselves growing continually in the qualities that we cherish most, then our life has meaning. We feel inner progress. We have direction, we have purpose. We become active and conscious participants in the life-game.

Let's spend some time now in the actual process of meditation. Allow me to begin by saying what meditation is *not*. Meditation is *not* thinking. People often have the image of Rodin's "The Thinker", in deep profound thought, when they anticipate meditation. Actually the best meditation, the highest states of meditation, take place in the complete absence of thought—in fact, not only the complete absence of thought but the complete absence of "mind".

The absence of mind is, I know, a difficult concept. We are so mind-dependent in perceiving and evaluating our world that awareness or experience without the mind operating is almost inconceivable. Let me paint a picture that may help.

Consider a bright light that is covered by a multi-coloured globe. If you did not know there was a light source inside,

Concentration & Meditation

Sri Chinmoy in soulful concentration

it would *appear* upon initial glance that the globe itself is emitting all those colours. But closer examination reveals that this is not the case at all. In fact, the globe emits no light whatsoever. The true source of light is inside the globe. The globe is simply filtering the true light through its various colours.

In exactly the same way, while the mind appears to have its own light, in fact, the mind has no light of its own; it is merely filtering the light that is emanating from the inner source. Just as you can remove the multi-coloured globe to experience the true source of light beneath it, so can you remove the "filtering" mechanism of the mind to get to the true source of all experience: the pure, undifferentiated consciousness-light of the soul. As you do so, the experience of inner light becomes purer and purer, brighter and brighter. In fact, a genuine meditative experience, regardless of the style or technique used, always comes with the perception that you are indeed experiencing a "higher" or "deeper" reality.

Let's face it, achieving this level of silent mind is equated with a somewhat advanced state of meditation. Most of us have difficulty enough just getting the mind to sit still for a few seconds! So, the first step of meditation begins with simply practicing quieting and focusing the mind, the step called concentration. It's not easy, but just because it's not easy doesn't mean it's not worth doing. Concentration means making the mind, and ultimately the entire being, completely one-pointed or focused.

Fortunately, it's not essential for the mind to be *absolutely* quiet to begin experiencing meditation. Imagine that you want to enjoy the vastness of the empty sky, but there are some birds passing through the sky. Well, the birds will only prevent you from enjoying the sky if you allow them to catch your attention as they go by. Similarly, in the process of seeking a one-pointed and still mind, should thoughts come, as they inevitably will in the beginning, simply let them pass by—don't be *mindful* of the mind's activities.

Approach concentration in reasonable steps. Think of the mind as a turbulent lake. Our first goal may be to simply calm the waves. Then we might try to make the mind-lake perfectly still.

Exercise / The mind's concentration

Earlier we used a candle to serve simply as a starting point for watching the actions of the mind. This exercise is similar to the very first exercise introduced on page 46, but here the emphasis should be on your concentration. You'll use the candle again, but this time deliberately **concentrate** on the candle flame. Try not to be distracted by any sounds. Sit comfortably erect in a chair or on the floor. The posture should encourage you not to be stiff, but simply alert. Your hands can sit comfortably on the lap. Try to allow no other thought, nothing else but the flame, to come into your mind. Simply place the mind at the flame. Do this for three to five minutes. While you're doing it, observe yourself. Take gentle note of what happens. What do you experience? What do you see? How do you change? Do your perceptions of the room and those around you change? Do you see things differently? Ultimately, do not lose sight of the goal—to make the mind absolutely one-pointed at the candle flame.

Were you able to absolutely quiet the mind? If you were, you are a member of a rare but fortunate breed. Most people only get glimpses of an absolutely quiet mind. After a brief silence visit, the mind chirps in, "Hey, you're doing it!" and then, of course, you're not anymore. That's interesting. After all, the mind is your mind, isn't it? Why is it that when you request the mind to be quiet, it doesn't cooperate? One of the first things we discover is that the mind has a mind of its own! I find this, I confess, a little sad. Earlier, we observed that the mind is constantly on the run, and now we see that not only is the mind on the run, but also that the mind has a mind of its own.

> Concentration wants to penetrate into the object it strives for. Meditation wants to live in the vastness of silence. — s.c.

Let's make some observations

Although subtle, perhaps the most important observation is that in spite of getting a glimpse at a non-thought state, you're still alive and well! Obviously then, who you are is not what the mind "thinks". It was Descartes who said, "Cogito ergo sum"—I think, therefore I am. (I say, "I think, ergo I worry!") Happily, we've just borne witness that even without thought we still exist. Existence and thought are *not* the same thing.

In order to make the mind quiet, we have to call upon something other than the mind to do it. We have to go deeper, and then impose our "will" on the mind. You have to say to the mind "shhhh!" and then, when it roams, keep bringing it back. Cultivating this will is an important part of taming the mind.

In the course of making the mind quiet and one-pointed, people usually experience some kind of perceptual changes. Allow me to review some of these, and see if you fit in somewhere.

Probably the most common observation is that the periphery of the room "fogs out", or disappears. Only the flame remains obviously visible. This occurs even in a well-lit room.

Another common observation is that the perception of the flame itself changes. The aura of the flame becomes more obvious. Some comment that the flame appears brighter, larger, or seems to come closer. Many say that the flame seems to move with their breathing, or they feel the warmth of the flame.

Some people become more aware of their own breathing, its sound and rhythm, and that it seems to have become steadier. Sometimes the comment is made that the body becomes more relaxed. Some will say that they can hear their joints creaking!

> " In concentration, you endeavour to bring the consciousness of your object right into your own awareness. In meditation, you rise from your limited consciousness into a higher and wider domain. ❧ s.c.

With regard to outside noises, commonly the low-grade "ground level" sounds fade out, while louder noises, like a background fan running or music playing appear to get louder.

Finally, I always poll my classes to determine if concentrating is a positive, peaceful experience or not. Typically, 19 out of 20 say "yes," while the rest find it otherwise, usually because they are frustrated with their inability to quiet the mind. Some actually experience tension.

Let's see if we can understand these responses. First of all, they are all the result of some individual change in perception. Obviously, the room doesn't disappear. The candle flame doesn't come any closer. These are all perceptual changes that occur with just a little effort to make the mind one-pointed.

Secondly, *these changes in perception are all attributable to some degree of success at concentrating!* When you concentrate on something, you are focusing in on the object of your concentration.

> Concentration wants to seize the knowledge it aims for. Meditation wants to identify itself with the knowledge it seeks for.
>
> ⚝ s.c.

You're no longer concerned with the myriad inputs to which the mind is usually only too happy to respond. Typically, the mind is constantly on the roam, and now you're saying to the mind, "Hey, focus here."

So, it's quite natural that you should become more "conscious" of the object you are concentrating on. When you concentrate on something, there's a mingling of consciousness between you and the object of your concentration. You become more aware of its existence and nature.

By extension, can you imagine the possibility of concentrating on something so completely and perfectly that the perception of duality disappears? It can be done. No longer will it be the candle and you, but the candle (or whatever the object) becomes an extension of your own consciousness.

This is a very advanced state of concentration. Great spiritual Teachers can do this. They can fully identify by extending their consciousness. But even at the beginner's level this extension of one's consciousness into the object of concentration expresses itself when the observer perceives that the candle seems brighter, closer or larger.

The aura around the candle becomes more obvious. In fact, the aura is always there, but by focusing on the candle and tuning out what you're not interested in, you can see it more readily. Similarly, the room seems to get darker because you're not concerned about the room. You have made a conscious effort to deny the extraneous input.

Eliminating some of the extraneous, non-essential input leaves only the very important or obvious input to be observed. People become aware of their breathing or body; louder noises seem to get louder. Obviously, the noise doesn't get louder, it just seems that way. In spite of this, people typically comment that they are actually less bothered by the noise.

> **It is** the work of concentration to clear the roads when meditation wants to go either deep within or high above.
> — S.C.

The mind is often compared to a lake. When the lake is turbulent, it becomes clouded and murky. The bottom of the lake can't be seen because the turbulence prevents this. Throw a small pebble into a turbulent lake and there seems to be no effect at all. But if the lake is calm, then it is clear. Throw a pebble into a calm lake and the ripples are apparent. When our minds are calm, we see more clearly and are much more sensitive to subtler input.

Finally, it is noteworthy that simply quieting the mind a little, even for first-timers, creates a sense of peace. Turning down the volume of the mind just a bit allows us to dwell in a calmer inner space. Some people *do* experience a tension in their heads when doing this. This comes from an inherent resistance from the mind itself. The mind behaves like a horse that has been allowed to roam freely. When you get on the horse for the first time to ride in a particular direction, what does the horse do? It bucks; it resists your instruction. So it might be with the mind. When you try to ride it in a particular direction, that is, when you concentrate, it may resist, creating a kind of tension in the mind, a "tug of war" between our intention to keep the mind quiet and the mind's unwillingness to listen to that intention.

> Concentration smilingly and blessingfully asks me: "O seeker, do you want to accomplish ten most significant things in the short span of ten minutes, or do you want to accomplish only one thing?" I tell concentration that I would like to accomplish ten most significant things in the short span of ten minutes. Concentration blessingfully and proudly tells me: "Then come and be in my boat. I am your only boatman."
>
> — s.c.

If you experienced any of these things to any extent, you've begun the process of concentration. Perhaps you experienced something else that wasn't mentioned. I'll leave it to you to explain it within the framework of our definition of concentration.

If you couldn't concentrate at all, don't fret. Think of the body. We understand that with proper diet and exercise, we can go from being "out of shape" to fit. So it is with the mind. With appropriate and regular exercise, we can take a cluttered, undisciplined mind and make it fit, focused, clear and sharp.

The ability to concentrate is a very, very beneficial tool, not only for learning to meditate (for which it is an essential first step) but also for life in general. When you can learn to really focus, you can bring that capacity to all your activities. So many of the benefits commonly associated with meditation—requiring less sleep, concentrating better, getting more work done, performing better at sport and other activities—come from the simple ability to concentrate and focus your attention/consciousness. Those of you who are students, or anyone who's a reader, knows the experience of having to re-read a paragraph over and over because while you're reading, the mind is somewhere else!

Concentration is the first step to recapturing your mind, making it yours. It should be practised regularly, every day. You will witness yourself getting better and better at it and, at the same time, will see yourself becoming more and more focused in your daily activities. You will conserve energy and have more time for important or new activities.

Remember that when you concentrate there is a "mingling" of consciousness between you and the object of your concentration. You can anticipate this when you direct your concentration to something that has a spiritual connotation for you—God, your heart or your spiritual ideal or Teacher—you'll begin to merge with that spirituality. You will experience an enlarged sense of consciousness, like a drop of water falling into the ocean. You will gradually merge into meditation. Concentration is the first rung on the meditation ladder.

> " Concentration and the surface mind dislike each other. Concentration opens the door to higher states of consciousness, while the surface mind wants to stay where it has always been. ✺ s.c.

From concentration to meditation

The divide between concentration and meditation is not hard and fast. Rather, one merges into the other. Remember that in concentration there is a projection of one's consciousness into the object of concentration. Now, if the object is something that embodies a much vaster consciousness, such as the soul, a spiritual ideal or one's spiritual Teacher, then, as you enter into that object, your consciousness expands into meditation.

Consider a drop of water falling into an ocean. Upon touching the ocean, it immediately expands to merge its identity with the ocean. So it is with concentration and meditation. When your concentration touches your infinite aspect, you expand into meditation. Herein lies the difference. In concentration, your consciousness is one-pointed, like a laser beam. In meditation, your consciousness expands to become the sun itself.

> The mind is division: world-division and self-division... The heart is acceptance: acceptance of the inner life and acceptance of the outer life. The inner life is aspiration. The outer life is dedication. — s.c.

Now, let's try to get a glimpse of the meditation experience. Remember, meditation does not happen in the mind. Meditation happens in the heart—the spiritual heart.

The heart, of course, is famous in spiritual literature. To reiterate a concept I spoke of before, just think of the heart as another room. The mind and heart are two different rooms inside our being. In life, if we want to eat, we might go from the living room to the kitchen. If we want to meditate, we want to leave the mind room and enter into the heart room.

Exercise / The heart's concentration

We're going to focus on the candle again, but this time we're going to use the heart as opposed to the mind. Again, the emphasis should be on your concentration.

When we use the mind, we say we are "thinking". What do you do when you use your heart? Feel. Feel love, feel compassion, feel oneness. This time, when you focus on the candle flame, do so with a sense of "loving" the candle, or perhaps, offering your goodwill from the heart. Try it and see.

● ● ●

Sit comfortably erect in a chair. With eyes closed, invite your mind into calm. Tell the mind that for just seven minutes you'd like to focus on the heart. For these seven minutes, nothing else matters save for your heart awareness. Envision, perhaps, a huge, calm ocean of peace in the mind extending outward in all directions with yourself at the centre. With each inhalation, imagine all the issues of your mind dissolving into this ocean.

First, begin by saying to yourself, "I am the heart." Simply say that to yourself. And recall for a moment your inner occupation, which is to grow into peace, joy or whatever inner quality appeals to you. Feel inside your heart a childlike cry to grow into peace, grow into light, grow into love.

Now bring your concentration to your breath. With each inhalation, follow the inhaling breath. Feel the air enter your nose, pass through your throat and enter the centre of your chest. Use the inhaling breath as a vehicle to drop out of the mind and fall into the middle of the chest. Try to centre your self-awareness there.

With each inhalation, feel yourself diving deeper and deeper into your heart.

Your eyes are still closed. Imagine yourself turning your vision inward into the heart. In a moment you'll open your eyes and, when you do so, feel as if your eyes are in your heart and your vision is coming from the inmost recesses of your heart.

Now, gently half open your eyes and look at the candle flame. Try to feel your heart's identification, your heart's oneness with the flame. Do this for three or four minutes; concentrate from your heart.

After a few minutes, close your eyes again and try to envision the candle flame in your heart which is perfectly still. See its light and feel its warmth. Do this for a few minutes.

Once more, open your eyes and bring your heart's awareness to the flame as you did earlier. Again, after three minutes, close your eyes and see the flame in your heart. This time, with each inhalation imagine the flame growing taller and brighter. It remains rooted in your heart but is climbing upwards toward the crown of your head with each inhalation. After a few minutes, imagine the light from the flame extending outward beyond the limits of your body—forward, backward, upward, downward, to the left and to the right. Let the light expand outward to fill the room you are in. Then take it beyond the limits of the room. Finally, take it to the limits of your imagination—upwards to the sky, outwards toward the horizon.

As a final part of this meditation, imagine that you want to find the source of this all-pervading light, that source being in the depths of your heart. Direct your vision inward and dive as deep as you can into your heart, seeking the root of the flame. After a few minutes more, open your eyes but keep all your focus rooted inside your heart.

If you are like most, this experience is very different from mental concentration. The room appears quieter and calmer. The body is relaxed. You feel much more free and peaceful. This is the experience of the heart.

It is very important to note that, in fact, nothing in the world around you has changed. The traffic is still flowing. The background noise is still there. The only thing that changed was you. You experienced a change in consciousness. You moved on down the fulfilment line.

This is the experience of the heart. If you didn't get it, no harm. There are many other techniques for you to try. If you did succeed, the task becomes to open this channel to the heart so that you can access it throughout the entire day, not just for the few minutes of the day when you sit for meditation. You'll quickly discover that the world takes on a completely different appearance when viewed through the heart of oneness as opposed to the mind of separation.

> O my mind-traveler,
> You cannot go very far.
> Your vision is very narrow.
> O my heart-traveler,
> The length and breadth of the world
> Are too narrow for you,
> For you far transcend
> The length and breadth of the world.
>
> s.c.

We begin meditation with the anticipation that meditation is somehow, some way going to affect our lives—and this is absolutely true. You can encourage this process along by knowing a little bit more about what makes you "you".

Sri Chinmoy describes the sum total of the human personality in a very interesting way and, when you see this model, I think you'll recognize yourself there. This inner psyche, the inner personality, your character, the thing that makes you "you", actually consists of an inner core surrounded by four different layers or sheaths of consciousness. I refer to this life model as a "cosmic onion" because, like an onion, the sheaths can be peeled away to reveal the core. A bull's-eye also works, as drawn on the next page.

The Cosmic Onion: Holistic Meditation

I'll begin by simply naming the sheaths, and then later describe the role they play. The innermost core of our being is the soul—the animating element. Recall that this is the term that I am using here, but you can refer to it by any term with which you are comfortable—Self, Inner Pilot, Atman, Spirit, whatever.

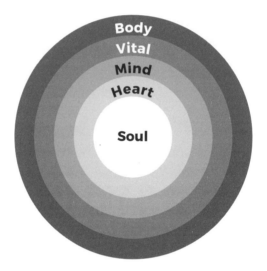

The soul abides in a particular room, and that room is the heart room. The heart is the most immediate sheath to the soul. Herein lies the significance of the spiritual heart. Because of its immediacy to the soul, the heart is essentially inundated with the soul's consciousness-light. We meditate in the heart, but it is actually the **soul** that we seek.

Surrounding the heart is the **mind**, or mental sheath. Then comes what Sri Chinmoy refers to as the **vital** sheath. And finally we have the physical, or the **body**.

The sum total of our human psyche consists of these various layers. Each of these layers has a different personality and sphere of influence of its own. Furthermore, depending on whether we're on the "wave-separate-desire" side of the consciousness line or the "ocean-oneness-aspire" side, the different sheaths of our being express themselves in different ways.

Interestingly, the personalities of the different sheaths can often be in conflict with each other. This often causes us to have arguments with ourselves! Who hasn't had the experience of "feeling" like doing one thing while "wisdom" advises to do something else? You know the proverbial "I *feel* like doing this, but I *know* I shouldn't!" Why this happens, and how meditation will help sort things out, will become clear as we proceed.

> "The vital aspires through dynamism. The mind aspires through self-search. The heart aspires through the feeling of union. The soul aspires through the perfection of God's manifestation.
>
> S.C.

We'll start with the outermost sheath, the body, and work our way inward.

The Body

To understand the body, let's explore a most interesting phenomenon—death. With death, the source of consciousness (the soul) departs and ultimately the body reverts back to mineral, its essential elements. It becomes rock-like again.

When I attended chiropractic school, for two years I studied and worked in the cadaver lab. It was a very interesting experience. I first anticipated the experience with a sense of curiosity and angst, but when I encountered my cadaver friends (there were 36 in the lab), my reaction was quite different. Here were all these body parts, but there was no life. I remember thinking, "If you put all the parts together, you still don't have life." It became absolutely clear that the body itself is not life at all, but simply the vehicle for life. The question occurred to me,

"What happens at that moment called death? What happens that makes all this flesh that was once warm, flowing and flexible, amazingly stop and, in a matter of minutes, become like a rock?" Consciousness leaves, and the suppleness of life leaves. Clearly, life is more than the summation of body parts.

Recall that consciousness is the fragrance or emanation of the soul. The less consciousness there is in the body, the less expression of the soul there is in the body and the more rock-like and inert it becomes. The unconscious body, at its worst, is flexible, mobile stone. It is lethargic. In fact, if I had to live my life purely according to the dictates of my body, what two things would I do? I have posed this question to every class that I have given and the answer is always the same: sleep and eat.

> My body wants to sleep.
> My vital wants to run.
> My mind wants to know.
> My heart wants to grow.
> My soul wants to glow.
> My Lord Supreme
> wants to flow. — s.c.

Most of us would like to think of ourselves as being motivated by higher ideals than these basic body issues. I ask you to sincerely reflect for a moment on your daily routine. Considering that the unconscious body's agenda is to sleep and eat, how much of your daily time do you spend planning your meals and relaxation time versus planning your meditation? I'll confess, if I spent as much time eating spiritual food as I do physical food, I'd be much more spiritually advanced and a lot thinner! I use this as motivation to plan my meditation by thinking of it as spiritual food and noshing as often as I can*.

You don't have to go any further than this to understand that the different sheaths of your being will express different and

---

* With regards to my own sleep-eat issues, I often joke that I practise "yen" meditation. Sometimes in my meditation I'll get an anticipation of some food, and I'll spend the rest of the day fulfilling that yen!

often conflicting needs. As my Teacher, Sri Chinmoy prescribes that I should be up meditating at six o'clock every morning. I find that when I do meditate with regularity and punctuality at that time, it helps my meditation tremendously. Knowing this doesn't change my morning ritual. My alarm goes off at 5:30 in the morning. Do you think I just pop out of bed, tiptoe over to my meditation shrine and start meditating? I hope I don't disappoint you in confessing that this is not what happens. No, not even after 40 plus years of meditating.

What does happen is this: the alarm goes off, I open my eyes and I immediately get a message, "Okay, get up and meditate." Then, another message immediately argues, "Oh man, you went to bed at 2 o'clock in the morning, you really should sleep for another hour or two." The first message is coming from my heart, and it repeats, "No, no, get up and meditate." The second message is coming from my body and it adds a great argument, "Hey, actually this whole week you've been really wiped out. Stay in bed." This tug of war between different parts of my being happens just about every morning.

Of course, I am hearing this debate inside my mind. So, the mind is receiving one message from the heart and another from the body. But often the mind has its own request list which it injects into the argument. The mind will say something like, "You've got so many things to do today. You'd better get out of bed." Or, alternately I may take the covers and throw them over my head because I don't want to face that list of responsibilities. Gratefully, most of the time my heart wins the battle**.

** *In my attempts to reduce my sleep need, I started to sleep on the floor to make sleep less comfortable. But instead, what happened is that since I learned how to sleep on the floor, I can now sleep anywhere including—are you ready?— standing up!*

(It's an interesting exercise in self-discipline to cut this whole morning ritual off at the start. We all know we're going to get out of bed eventually, so when you wake up in the morning and hear the mind start to generate all its stuff, just nip it in the bud. Don't get involved in the conversation. Get up. You'll gain valuable time in the day. Turning the lights on is the trick. Once the lights are on, you'll wake up. Invest in a timer to turn the lights on, or buy the clapper!)

> My body cries.
> My vital sighs.
> My mind fears.
> My heart hesitates.
> My soul wanders.
> My Lord Supreme wonders.
>
> s.c.

So you see, the first thing in the morning, my message centre starts. Already, different parts of my being are giving me different messages, and this continues throughout the day. Is it any wonder that we often feel conflicted when making decisions? Meditation has an interesting impact on all this, as you'll see in just a bit.

Now, back to the body. On the desire side of the consciousness continuum, the body is lethargic and inertial. On the aspiration side of the consciousness spectrum, the body has a different role. Recall that earlier I suggested that our primary nature is spiritual and we are meant to express that spirituality through the physical. The body is intended to be a vehicle through which the soul expresses itself. It's said that the body is the "temple" and the soul is the "shrine inside the temple". It's said that the body is the "chariot" and the soul is the "charioteer". The body is the immediate vehicle for spiritual expression and manifestation.

◉ The Vital

The next sheath is the vital. The vital is perhaps the most difficult sheath to describe, but it's the easiest one to experience. Most of the basic emotional and sensual experiences that we have in life are vital experiences. I call the vital the "colouring agent" in common life.

Let me give an example to make it clear. Suppose while walking to work you pass by the local Baskin & Robbins ice cream store. You decide that after work, you'll trek to that Baskin & Robbins to order an extra-thick chocolate malted made with French vanilla ice cream. (Highly recommended. Be sure to tell the vendor that price is no object.) Now, if after work you simply affirm your decision to do this and then move the body to do so, order your malted and drink it down, you've used the mind to make the decision and the body to perform the action.

That would be pretty boring and, of course, that is not what really happens. Between your decision and your action comes all this emotional anticipation. "Oh God, I can't wait to get there. Can I sample this one first? Mmmm, is this good!" A major portion of this anticipation comes from the vital. The vital colours our life experience sensually and emotionally.

Now, on the desire side of the consciousness spectrum, the vital tends to be aggressive in nature. Remember all the superiority/inferiority issues associated with the wave end of the spectrum? [See page 100] They are, for the most part, vital emotions. The vital wants to grab onto the world and say, "Hey, this is mine!" Sri Chinmoy said that the unillumined vital is epitomised by the famous utterance of Julius Caesar, "Veni, vidi, vici"—I came, I saw, I conquered.

> " My body will see.
> My vital will feel.
> My mind will believe.
> My heart will realise.
> My soul will smile.
> My Lord Supreme will rest.
> ⁓ S.C.

On the illumined side of the consciousness spectrum, the vital is dynamic and creative. It wants to work, serve and create. This movement from the desire side to the oneness side of the consciousness spectrum represents a transition and a transformation—a transformation into selflessness. For the vital sheath, this transformation represents a change from an aggressive energy that is trying to grab and possess the world, to a selfless, dynamic and creative energy that is trying to offer itself and serve the world. When I introduced Sri Chinmoy, I noted that he'd painted 140,000 paintings and drawn 16 million birds. This is the soul's inspiration operating through an illumined vital. It's something that we all have at our disposal. The illumined vital colours our lives with a host of higher emotions, all based on the experience of oneness.

◉ The Mind

We've already spent some time exploring the mind's nature. The mind is the decision-maker and the investigator. It wants to know, but its method of knowing changes, however, depending on which side of the consciousness spectrum it is positioned. The unillumined mind, as we've observed, knows through separating, criticising, analysing. I will add doubting. It constantly questions, "Why?" Left to its own, at its best it imposes upon itself a framework of logic and reason. Allow me to emphasise the word *impose*. Logic and reason are rarely the primary operating modes of the mind. We can choose those modes, should we want to. But more often, the mind calls upon its collected data banks and allows itself to be influenced by the unillumined vital and body consciousness to ultimately make its choices.

> My mind
> Always loves to be
> The curiosity-devourer.
> My heart
> Loves to be the collector
> Of God's golden Dreams.
>
> ✄ S.C.

On the illumined side of the spectrum, logic is replaced by intuition. The mind becomes faith-filled. The mind has vision. It remains the decision-maker but on the illumined side it becomes the true discriminator—between truth and non-truth, between right and wrong. Why and how this transformation occurs in the mind will become clear when I finish the model.

◉ The Heart

The heart, for the most part, is associated with the illumined side of the spectrum. Recall that the soul resides inside the heart room, and it is by virtue of this intimacy that the heart is almost completely identified with the illumined side of the spectrum. Allow me to revise the original onion diagram to appear as shown below.

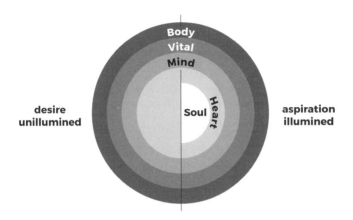

There are moments when the heart does associate itself with the unillumined side, at which time it expresses itself as insecurity. It feels lost by virtue of its separation from its own highest reality. But for all practical purposes, and certainly for the purpose of this discussion, the heart is completely identified with the illumined side of the consciousness spectrum. The illu-

> To make the fastest progress in my spiritual life, I need a mind watchful, a heart soulful and a breath Godful.
>
> ✖ s.c.

mined heart has many qualities associated with it—compassion, tolerance, oneness. But undoubtedly its most significant expression is in selfless or unconditional love.

The need to love and to feel loved is, perhaps, the dominant influence in most people's lives. We use the word "love" day in and day out in our conversation, but I sincerely feel love to be a sacred thing. Sadly, the love that most of us experience is rarely unconditional and therefore should not be considered love at all, in the purest sense of the term. The typical "human" love experience begins with need and is an expression of the unillumined vital. Most people seek a loving relationship with someone because they feel empty, needful. Something is missing in their lives, so they seek love from a position of weakness.

> The Promised Land is for him who perpetually lives in the widening pastures of the soul. ❧ s.c.

The human love experience is often one of mutual need fulfilment and is therefore subject to the rules which operate in any desire. The experience changes when those needs are not fulfilled appropriately. Swami Vivekananda referred to human love as "marketing".

It is not my intention to denigrate the human love experience but only to clarify how it is different from the unconditional love of the heart. It is not the nature of the heart to love some**one** or some**thing** but rather to be **all** loving. The unconditional love of the heart does not ask, "Hey, I offered you love—did you get it? And what do I get in return?" No, it is truly selfless, truly unconditional and, as such, is its own fulfilment. The love of the spiritual heart is said to be self-amorous. That is, it loves and, in so doing, feels fulfilled at being loved.

◉ The Soul

Finally, at the core of our being is the soul, spirit or self. It is the animating element. It gives life. It is that aspect of the universal consciousness or of God that exists inside each of us.

The soul, of course, is the essence. Please allow me to defer to Sri Chinmoy in speaking about the soul. This writing comes from his book Songs of the Soul. This book was one of the first books I read as Sri Chinmoy's student, and it remains one of my favorites. I re-read it regularly.

> "To perfect our human life, by far the greatest necessity is our soul's delight. When we live in the physical, the teeming clouds of desire are natural, necessary and inevitable. When we live in the soul, the ever-mounting flames of aspiration are natural, necessary and inevitable.
>
> When we live in the soul, we spontaneously cultivate God. His Peace, Bliss and Power become ours, absolutely ours. We grow into our spiritual perfection. This perfection is at once our divine heritage in a human body and our unearthly birthright on earthly soil.
>
> The human in us must live under the sheltering wings of the soul. The divine in us must fly and fly into the Beyond with the flying wings of the soul. The human in us must eventually need transformation. The divine in us must eventually need manifestation...

(Songs of the Soul, "Man Immortalised")

Change your mind!

Let's step back to take hold of how this life-model works. On the desiring side, we have the body, vital and mind operating. *(Refer back to the diagram on page 125.)* Here, for the most part, the mind serves as the senior member. Of course, there are times when one may make a decision based purely on vital or physical need, but it is generally true that on the desiring side, the mind is the captain.

Drawing on the earlier descriptions, the body-vital-mind model doesn't make a very pretty picture—we have a separating, criticising, analytical, doubting mind using this aggressive vital to motivate an inert, lethargic body. I am not being judgmental here. Everyone, certainly myself included, has this side of the consciousness range operating at some time.

But, on the aspiring side, we have the body, vital, mind, heart and soul operating. Note that the position of the mind goes through the most dramatic change. On the aspiring side, the mind is situated between its two younger family members, the body and the vital, and its two older family members, the heart and the soul. With that change in position, the mind assumes a very different role. Consider my morning wake-up ritual. That entire debate is happening inside my mind. The mind receives input from its elder brothers, the heart and soul: "Get up and meditate." It also receives input from the younger members of the inner family, the body and vital, "Stay in bed."

Without the heart and soul operating, the mind is left to its own tools to make decisions—reason, logic, doubt, analysis and curiosity—as influenced by the demands of the vital and body. On the aspiring side, the mind is receiving input from above—the heart and soul, and input from below, the vital and body, and it strikes a balance. Sometimes, it strikes a balance in the direction of the junior members of the being (I stay in bed), and sometimes it strikes a balance in the direction of the senior members of the being (I get up and meditate). On the illumined side, the mind is positioned to receive the necessary input it needs to make the appropriate decision. What is "appropriate" ultimately is determined by the result of the decision—I learn from the positive response that it is wiser for me to get up as opposed to staying in bed. Slowly and steadily, the mind becomes reconditioned to listen to and trust the heart.

Ultimately, I ask the mind to completely surrender its role as decision-maker to the heart. This process takes place as the heart becomes more self-evident, and we bear witness to its wisdom in our lives.

It is by virtue of the new input from the senior members of the inner family that the mind becomes more intuitive. When the heart and soul are not operating, *the mind has no choice but to operate, at best, by reason, or to surrender to the influences of the vital and body*; that's its only mode of operating. It says, "yes, no, yes, no"; it determines things logically or succumbs to desire.

But when meditation opens up the heart channel, the mind gets a higher and subtler input. New faculties of the mind begin to develop. In essence, it is receiving more inner light and with this inner light comes improved vision. We gain insight and understanding to the underpinnings of our life interactions. Inner wisdom develops. Slowly but surely, reason and knowledge become tempered by vision, wisdom and intuition.

> "With an eager heart
> I have been waiting
> For my mind's transformation.
> With a smiling heart
> I shall continue to wait
> Until my mind's transformation
> dawns. ➴ s.c.

With the cultivation of the heart and consequential inclusion of the heart into our character, we operate much more holistically. We are more complete human beings. Fact accumulation is replaced by vision-wisdom-intuition. Our base emotions are replaced by higher, more fulfilling emotions. The body becomes an instrument instead of a weight. All of this happens under the loving guidance of the heart—we become whole.

Once again, allow me to defer to Sri Chinmoy. These writings again all come from *Songs of the Soul*.

My Body

❝O my body, you are a gift of the Supreme. Potentiality inexhaustible you have, deep within you. To misunderstand you means to misunderstand the chosen instrument of God.

You want not, you must not, you cannot conquer the length and breadth of the world with your physical strength. Offer your growing heart to the hearts far and near. Offer your glowing soul to the souls around, below, above. Then alone you become the conqueror and possessor of God's entire universe.

O my body, invoke your soul always for you to lead. Invoke! Never shall the monotony of the uneventful life plague you. With lightning speed yours shall be the ceaseless march . . . upward to the Highest, inward to the Inmost, forward to the Farthest.

Sing, sing the song of Bliss in Immortality! Breathe, breathe in the breath of Consciousness in Immortality! Live, live the life of Existence in Immortality!

Death? Die you must not. For your death will be a great loss to humanity and by far a greater loss to Divinity. Fight, O my body, fight with ignorance to the bitterest end. Never allow ignorance to envelop you, your outer cloak. Your tearing efforts shall be crowned with success.

O body of mine, fare you well for eternity. May each earthly year of yours have a trillion fulfilling years.

God the Eternal Dreamer is dreaming through you, with you. God the Eternal Reality is living for you, with you and in you.

(Songs of the Soul, "My Body")

My Vital

O my vital, my first choice falls on you. Without your dynamic and stupendous inner urge, nothing can be embodied, nothing can be revealed here on earth.

O my vital, when you fall fast asleep, my mind's undying frustration grips my outer existence. My body's helpless surrender to the Prince of Gloom poisons my inner existence.

Man's most powerful imagination fails to fathom you, your depth. Man's far-flung, brightest wisdom fails to determine you, your breadth.

Yours is the indomitable courage that springs from the fountain of boundless emotion. Kill not your emotion, never. Emotion killed within, fulfilment starved without. Emotion divinely fed within, God the Eternal Delight revealed without.

O my vital, you know no Tomorrow. You want to be born, you want to grow and fulfil yourself in the immediacy of Today. With the infinite Blessings of the Supreme, on you march across the path of Infinity's bloom, Eternity's glow and Immortality's lustre.

Your life is green, the ever-aspiring and ever-growing green. Your breath is blue, the ever-encompassing and ever-transforming blue.

O vital of mine, in you is humanity's glowing Hope. With you is Divinity's reverberating Clarion.

(Songs of the Soul, "My Vital")

My Mind

"O my mind, no earthly chain can fetter you. You are always on the wing. No human thought can control you. You are forever on the move.

O my mind, hard is it for you to believe in my soul's constant fulfilment. And hard is it for me to believe that you are doomed to be the eternal victim of venomous doubts. Alas! You have forgotten. You have forgotten the golden secret: "To remain in the Silence-Room is to open the Fulfilment-Door."

O my mind, vast are your responsibilities. You have to please your superiors: heart and soul. Only with your warmest admiration will you be able to conquer the heart. Only with your deepest faith will you be able to conquer the soul. You have also to satisfy your subordinates: the body and the vital. Only with your pure concern will you be able to make the body smile. Only with your genuine encouragement will you be able to help the vital run unmistakably towards good and not pleasure.

O my mind, I need you desperately, either to abide in you or to go beyond you. You see and thus protect the physical in me. You serve and thus reveal the spiritual beyond me.

O my mind, cast aside your long-treasured arid reason. Welcome the ever-virgin faith. Possess the naked sword of conscience. Far above the storms of fear you are destined to climb. Stay no more in self-created somber shadows of death. Don the golden robes of simplicity, sincerity and purity. Permit not the gales of disbelief to extinguish your inner mounting flame. Yours is the arrow of concentration. Yours is the soil of lightning intuition. Yours is the unhorizoned peace.

Behold the Supreme! He crowns you, O mind of mine, with the laurel of His infinite Bounty.

(Songs of the Soul, "My Mind")

My Heart

" *O my heart, I am divinely proud of you. You do not have the shameful and shameless disease—worry! Never do you drink the deadly venom—doubt! Nothing can be simpler than your pure long-ings. Nothing can be more spontaneous than your glowing feelings. Nothing can be more fulfilling than your selfless love. Nothing has a more immediate access to the Supreme than your inmost cry.*

O my heart, your heavenly day within an earthly day is for God-realisation. Your immortalising minute within a fleeting minute is for God-embodiment. Your revealing second within a vanishing second is for God-manifestation.

O my heart, the other members of the family are afraid of God. You are never! Their lightless persistent fear is a lifeless persistent para-lysis. In life's journey others make their own choice. God makes the choice for you. They want to save humanity with their ego's darkest night. You wish to serve humanity with your dedication's brightest day. Their victory is the victory over humanity. Your victory is the victory over yourself.

O my heart, O heart of mine, you are my life-boat. You sail the uncharted seas of ignorance and reach the golden shore of the Beyond.

I am not alone, O my heart, I am with your soaring aspiration. You are not alone. In you and for you is my life's unreserved breath.

Yours is the unfaltering Will and unfailing faith in the Supreme. Each petal of the radiant lotus deep within you is perpetually bathed in nectar-rays of the Transcendental Delight.

O sweet, sweeter, sweetest heart of mine, you are not only God's. God also is yours.

(Songs of the Soul, "My Heart")

My Soul

O Soul, I am your body.

I am thirty-six years old today. I wish to learn from you.

"Do good."

O Soul, I am your vital. I am nineteen years old. I want to learn from you.

"Be good."

O Soul, I am your mind. I am sixty years old. I need to learn from you.

"See good."

O Soul, I am your heart. I am four years old. Please tell me the secret.

"Remain good."

O Soul, your body again. What do you do with your boundless Love?

"I distribute my boundless Love to ever-expanding horizons."

O Soul, your vital again. What do you do with your Infinite Peace?

"I feed the teeming vasts of the Past, Present and Future with my Infinite Peace."

O Soul, your mind again. What do you do with your Vision of the ever-transcending Beyond?

"I feather the Golden Nest of my Reality's Infinitude with my Vision of the ever-transcending Beyond."

O Soul, once more your heart. Tell me your absolute secret, please.

"I live for the Supreme and for the Supreme alone. This is my Absolute Secret."

(Songs of the Soul, "My Soul")

Exercise / Meditation for the body, vital, mind and heart

As you know, I encourage you to fold your hands over your heart whenever you meditate. I find it helps in a number of ways. The very act of touching something helps to focus attention there. When you bruise yourself, typically you'll put your hand over that area which somehow seems to soothe the area. In a similar way, the simple act of touching your heart helps to draw your inner attention there.

Again, on a subtler level, I feel that when I fold my hands over my heart, two special qualities immediately present themselves: humility and devotion. These qualities help me in my meditation. This spiritual exercise was prescribed by Sri Chinmoy as a way to bring the necessary qualities into each area, and it takes advantage of hand placement to help bring attention to each.

Of course, begin with your ABCs. Sit erect and take a minute to affirm your spiritual intention. Make an inner contract with yourself that these next 10, 15, 20 or 30 minutes are dedicated to your inner life. For the first minute, allow yourself to feel that nothing is more important than your hunger for inner peace, light, joy, love, divinity.

When you are comfortably situated "within", place your right hand on the crown of your head and soulfully repeat the word "simplicity" to yourself. While repeating it, feel that your life is simplicity itself, unfettered by worldly problems or issues.

After a few minutes, place your hand over the "third eye", the point between and a little above the eyes. Repeat the word "sincerity" to yourself. Feel yourself to be the embodiment of sincerity.

Again, after a few minutes, move your hand over your heart. For a minute or two, repeat the word "surety" to yourself. Simultaneously, feel absolute confidence in your inner life of aspiration.

Finally, place your hand over the navel and repeat "purity" to yourself. As you repeat purity, feel all base emotions—anger, jealousy, pride—dissipating.

Exercise / Concentration variation

I like to do a variation of this using concentration as a vehicle to carry in/out those qualities which I want to incorporate/eliminate. At your meditation area, place before you a symbol of spiritual value. It can be the flame of a lighted candle, a flower, or, if you have a spiritual Teacher, by all means place a photo of your Teacher before you.

For one minute, while concentrating on your chosen object, feel that the mind is emptying itself through the third eye. Empty the mind of all thought. Do this for a minute or two. Then, imagine that sincerity of the highest order is entering your mind coming from your chosen symbol.

Then move to the heart. While concentrating on your chosen symbol, empty yourself of all insecurity and fear. Then feel that your heart is being filled with the sweetest love. Again, do this for a minute or two.

From the navel, empty yourself of all base emotions. Then imagine a golden light entering into the vital filling that entire area with purity. (Another minute or two.)

Finally, for the final few minutes of this exercise, imagine a white light entering into the crown of your head, filling your entire being with highest divinity.

Repeat this sequence two or three times. I often refer to this exercise as doing "meditation sprints"!

Ultimately, meditation can and should affect every part of your inner being. And because each layer has its own personality and set of issues, there are exercises and activities you can perform on a layer-by-layer basis that will help in the transition/transformation from the unillumined side to the illumined side. In essence, we can define a meditation for each layer that will make that layer more "receptive" to the spiritual process.

Consider the gardener. He could simply plant seeds and hope for the best. Alternatively, in addition to planting the seeds, the gardener could also till the soil, enrich the soil with proper nutrients, water the soil, remove any competing weeds and check his garden daily. Here the gardener is making his field more receptive and, in so doing, is much more likely to develop a bumper crop.

Let us examine each layer and determine how we can encourage receptivity.

Inner and Outer Development

Meditation for the body

Recall that the unillumined body tends toward lethargy and inertia and, in the course of its transformation, evolves to become the temple for the soul. We might ask, "How can we encourage the body in the direction of the illumined side?"

If the unillumined body is lethargic and inertial, then clearly if we impose movement on the body, we must be shifting toward the illumined side of the consciousness continuum. Disciplined, conscious movement, i.e. exercise, is meditation for the body! Although any one exercise session might be tiring, the fact is the more you exercise regularly, the more net energy you have. The converse of this is true as well, the less you exercise, the less energy you have.

You can verify this with anybody who exercises regularly. I can testify to this personally. As part of our spiritual discipline, Sri Chinmoy encourages his students to exercise regularly. In particular, he encourages us to run two miles a day.

Now, I am not by nature a runner. In fact, if you see me run, you might ask, "What is he doing?" I have invented a new running form. I call it "schlogging". There is a Yiddish word, "schlep", which means "to carry with a bit of a burden". For example, in an airport one might "schlep" their suitcase from terminal to terminal. Well, my running is half schlepping and half jogging, therefore, "schlogging".

When I schlog regularly, I have much more life energy. When I don't schlog or do any exercise, my body starts to feel like it's hanging on me.

I am often asked, "Why does Sri Chinmoy prefer running?" Sri Chinmoy suggests that the runner is a perfect metaphor for what we are trying to do inwardly—step-by-step, little by little, we should grow in peace, light, joy. We make progress one step at a time.

My own experience is that in running, only two things are operating: my body and my will to move the body. Since I am not a great runner, I do not find it aesthetically pleasing. I also swim and bike occasionally. Both of these have a pleasing aspect to them that I don't experience while running. Biking is swift. I can coast from time to time; I can be entertained by the passing scenery. Swimming simply feels good as the water flows past you. But running is just me and my will, so it doesn't surprise me to find a direct correlation between my regularity in running and my regularity in other disciplines that I practise. Even though my knees may ache, running is worth it.

But regardless of the exercise method, consciously performed exercise can be conscious-ness-raising, and I suspect that this fact is in part responsible for the exercise boom. Sure, we've all read about the endorphins that supposedly make you feel better, but I think it's simply that exercise makes the body more receptive to an inner light. Exercise is meditation for the body.

> " No matter how old you are, if you want to make progress in your spiritual life, if you want to make progress in your vital, mind, heart and soul, then physical fitness is absolutely necessary. If the physical fails, everything fails. The physical is the temple. If there is no temple, there can be no shrine. ⚘ s.c.

As a temple for the soul, we should keep the body healthy and strong with appropriate diet—not too strict but certainly not too indulgent either. A vegetarian diet is very helpful from both the health and the meditation standpoint.

A temple should not be unclean. Smoking, alcohol and drugs are very destructive to inner receptivity. I am not in any way suggesting that if you smoke, you can't meditate. But if you can stop, it will be of tremendous benefit. I don't know of a single smoker who has not at some time attempted to stop without success. Happily, many meditation students have confessed that after beginning meditation, they found it much easier to eliminate unhealthy habits such as smoking because they felt motivated from within by a higher purpose.

Here is our first glimpse of the outer and the inner relationship. We can exercise outwardly to make us more inwardly receptive, and we can meditate to help motivate or inspire us to make positive changes in our outer life.

Meditation for the vital

Recall the transition that takes place in the vital—from aggressive and desiring to creative, dynamic and serving. Therefore, to encourage the vital, we want to seek dynamic and creative outlets for vital expression. On a regular basis, immerse yourself in some activity that allows you to be selfless and creative. It could be art, it could be music, it could be weaving!

Personally I've found that it's a wonderful experience to cook for others. Please do not ignore the selfless aspect. Think in terms of serving others *without expecting anything in return*. That's the kicker. Exercise your selflessness! Provide your vital with a vehicle to use its energy in a pure and positive way to encourage the transition from the unillumined to the illumined.

Also, please recall that the vital has an emotional aspect to it. Most of our base emotions are based in the unillumined vital. Fortunately, there are higher and more fulfilling emotions associated with the illumined vital. Therefore, it behooves us to consciously work to transform the lower emotions and cultivate the higher emotions *(see page 169 for a discussion on transformation)*. Let anger give way to tolerance and oneness. Let impatience give way to determination and patience. Let pride give way to humility and gratitude.

Finally, with regard to the vital, it's important to acknowledge that many of the emotions associated with sexual expression are based in the unillumined vital as well. This energy, like everything else, needs to be redirected. I have found that many westerners get stuck here. This process is terribly misunderstood so I have dedicated a special section to it later in the book *(see page 172)*.

Meditation for the mind

I'm going to spend quite a bit of time here because so much of spiritual processing ultimately has to do with which part of the being dominates our life interaction, the mind or the heart. Recall from our previous discussion that, before one begins meditating, the mind is given license to be the leader of the inner family. This transition from being firstborn to middle child is not a transition that the mind readily makes. We begin the meditation process by asking the mind to be silent, something to which the mind is not at all accustomed. Because it has been allowed to roam freely for so long, it often demonstrates a reluctance to being disciplined. If you are one of those individuals who struggle with "I just can't concentrate," don't fret. Consider the body for a moment. Can you anticipate that with a good diet and solid exercise program, you can improve the body's fitness and strength? Of course. Well, in exactly the same way, with an appropriate diet and exercise program, you can take a restless undisciplined mind and make it focused, clear and strong.

Let's start with diet. The mind feeds itself on information. It makes sense to take advantage of this behaviour and feed the mind inspiring information. Reading spiritual writings should be part of a regular meditative lifestyle. These writings should be those of genuine spiritual Masters. I'm not suggesting reading spiritual writings to the exclusion of all other things, but by feeding the mind spiritual information, you are encouraging it to be a partner in the process of moving in a positive direction.

What else does the mind do? Obviously, it thinks. (No surprise here!) It is very, very important to redirect our thinking. This is not only extremely important, but valuable. So many times in classes, participants admit that they want to learn to meditate simply to escape the constant rambling of their minds. It is not merely the "busy-ness" of their minds, but the *quality* of the thoughts. Too often our minds are filled with worries, anxieties, angers, criticisms and doubts. The task is not merely to silence the mind, but also to improve the quality of the thoughts that we do experience when the mind is called upon. Remember, the mind can be disciplined in exactly the same way the body can be disciplined. You've simply got to put it on an exercise program!

Exercises for the mind

Although I am about to suggest a series of exercises for the mind, let me begin by reiterating the value of concentration. Concentration can be practised separately from your meditation proper, or it may be part of your meditation by concentrating on your heart, a spiritual ideal or a spiritual Teacher.

The following exercise is a simple yet effective exercise in concentration and projecting your consciousness. As a general rule, when you practise concentration, you want to focus on something as small as possible.

Exercise **/ Concentration on a dot**

There is merit in simply practising pure concentration for concentration's sake. You can add spiritual value by framing the purpose of your concentration with proper intent. In other words, approach this exercise with the thought, "I am practising my concentration to make my meditation more intense and pure."

On a piece of paper, draw a circle about three inches in diameter and place a small dot at the centre. The dot should be no smaller than the head of a pencil. Tape the paper to a wall so that the dot is just at seated eye level.

Sit two or three feet away from the wall and simply bring the full power of your concentration to the dot. Increase the power of your concentration so that you do not even see the circle, only the dot. When you accomplish this, imagine yourself passing through the dot and placing yourself on the other side of the dot!

The impact of concentration will not only improve your meditation, but also will positively affect virtually every aspect of your outer life, guaranteed!

The power of words

In addition to pure concentration, a number of other exercises for the mind, which I will suggest in a little bit, have a theme which is central to all of them—the power found in a word.

Words are valuable conveyers of meaning and this conveyance happens in two ways. Obviously, a word can be a "symbol" for some outer entity. We use the word "desk" to represent the table on which we perform our work. The word "sky" is that space above our head. But words also convey an *inner* meaning. Let's do a simple exercise to appreciate the inner meaning and effect of words.

Exercise / The inner meaning of words

Repeat each of the following words a few times and watch your inner reaction to them. Begin by taking a minute just to quiet yourself so you can better sense your inner response.

Now silently repeat the word "peace" a few times. When you repeat it, try to imagine that the word is being repeated not in your mind, but in your heart. Watch your response as you repeat it.

After a few minutes, silently repeat the word "bliss". Again, hear it in your heart for a minute or two, and watch your inner response.

Finally, only for a few seconds, repeat the following word: "cancer". Just do this for a few seconds and again, get a sense of your inner reaction.

If you are like most folks, repeating the word "cancer" is associated with a distinctively different inner reaction than "peace" or "bliss". Students in my classes typically describe their reaction with comments such as: "I shrink", "contracting", or "withdrawal".

It might be suggested that the effects created by the various words occur because of their outer associations and certainly this is, in part, true. But it also is true that each word has a "climate" about it, and when one repeats a word, one is affected by that inner climate. Every time we use a word, we make an investment in its inner climate or meaning. Let me explain.

Have you ever visited a temple, synagogue, church or mosque which has an especially profound inspiring effect on you—a place where you simply feel more peaceful or uplifted? If you ever have the wonderful opportunity to visit Japan, make sure to visit the Buddha statue at Kamakura. The peace there is so palpable, you feel like you are bathing in it. (On the following page is a photo of Sri Chinmoy meditating in front of the Kamakura Buddha.)

Now, not every temple affects you this way ... only those certain special places. Why is that so? I believe it is because of the investment of devotion that is made in the place. When people pray, meditate and chant devotedly and regularly in one particular place, their collective investment creates a solid palpable inner climate.

Words are the same way. The way in which we use a word outwardly creates an inner climate for that word. We can take advantage of this inner climate to affect how our minds behave and think. We use words to communicate outwardly and we use meditation to communicate inwardly. This relationship between word and spirituality, between sound and silence, is witnessed in historical theology. I find it more than curious that in the Christian teaching, the Book of John starts, "In the beginning was the word ... " and Hindu theology suggests that with the word "AUM" (pronounced OM), God set his universe in motion. Interesting, yes? *(See: AUM in the Appendix, page 257.)*

> " By chanting AUM, you can easily reveal inner and outer perfection, for AUM embodies the highest height and the deepest depth. AUM embodies Universal Consciousness, Transcendental Consciousness.
>
> S.C.

Sri Chinmoy meditating in front of the Daibutsu at Kamakura, Japan

◎ Japa, mantra, song

Because thoughts, which are composed of words, are constantly passing through the mind, we can use words to impose a discipline back on the mind. One of the oldest spiritual exercises is called "japa". Japa is the continual repetition of a word or group of words which have a spiritual climate (based on our discussion above). Such a word or group of words is called a "mantra". Mantra is Sanskrit and means "chant".

Choosing a mantra is not a casual thing. A personal mantra must be assigned to a student by a genuine Master. A proper mantra can never be assigned by proxy. But, if you don't have a spiritual Teacher, you can safely use the word "AUM" which is considered to be the mother of all mantras. "Shanti" (Sanskrit for peace), "Supreme", or "peace" can all be used as well.

Sri Ramakrishna explained japa something like this. He likened the mind to a bottle of ink. The repetition of a holy word, then, is like dropping clear water into the ink bottle. Drop-by-drop, eventually the content of the bottle becomes clear. Similarly, when japa is regularly performed, tremendous clarity and purity enters the mind.

Exercise / Performing japa

Sri Chinmoy recommends doing japa in a very specific way. Begin your japa at a regular time. Use either the word AUM or Supreme. You can chant as quickly as you like, but always soulfully and with concentration. (Soulfulness and speed can easily go hand-in-hand.) On the first day, silently repeat the mantra 500 times. Then for one week, on each succeeding day, add 100 repetitions until, a week later, you repeat the word 1,200 times. For the second week, decrease the number of repetitions by 100 each day until you are back to 500. Then again increase by 100 for a week and then decrease by 100 for a week.

Doing japa this way, Sri Chinmoy says, allows tremendous light and purity to enter into the mind, making the mind more fertile for spiritual receptivity. Again, he emphasises the importance of soulful repetition, meditative repetition, saying that it is better to repeat a word seven times with utmost soulfulness than it is to repeat it 100 times mechanically.

Now how do you keep count? Traditionally, japa is done using either your fingers to count, or by using a band of beads which have 100 (actually 108) beads on them, the last bead being larger. Using japa beads (or mala beads as they are also called) frees you from the task of counting. Those of you who were raised Catholic should recognize something here ... the Rosary is a form of japa.

> **"** The mantric power can easily take one to the Highest, as prayer and meditation do. Chanting a mantra is also a form of approaching God. It has its own efficacy and its own approach towards the Highest.
>
> S.C.

Exercise / Three minute chanting

This is a variation on traditional japa and it is one of my favorites. It also incorporates a little visualization as well.

This exercise involves three, three-minute periods. For the first three-minute period, silently chant "Supreme" to yourself as quickly as you possibly can. Imagine that you are trying to chase out all other thoughts—that you are trying to be saturated in the word "Supreme".

For the second three-minute period, again silently chant "Supreme" to yourself, but this time chant as slowly, soulfully, heartfully and prayerfully as you possibly can. Imagine every cell in your being is crying for the Supreme.

For the final three minutes, imagine that you are a child inside your own heart and you write the word "Supreme" on the wall of your spiritual heart. You can see it: S-U-P-R-E-M-E. Then concentrate on each letter, one at a time. First, concentrate on the "S" and imagine a luminous blue light emanating from the S. When you see this light, silently chant "Supreme" to yourself once. In this way, concentrate on each letter in succession.

Finally, after concentrating on each letter, chant "Supreme" aloud, soulfully and prayerfully seven times.

Song and music

Although I list music and song as exercises for the mind, music also illumines the vital and feeds the heart. Music and meditation are very closely related. Like meditation, music is a language which has ready access to our inner space. We invite music in quite deliberately to affect us in a desirable way. Calming music chills us out. We may play a more lively music to keep us alert. A simple melody can transport us back in time.

Different music affects us differently. Certain music is directed to the body and vital. For me, it's impossible to listen to Led Zeppelin's "Stairway to Heaven" without the old hippy coming to the fore. Without realizing it, my head is bopping up and down! Despite its name, "Stairway to Heaven" is not music to meditate by!

Devotional music is quite different. You see, the most important ingredient in music is a silent one—it is the consciousness of the performer. When music is created from the spiritual heart, it can be a source of tremendous inspiration.

Of course, song is a subset of music. Sri Chinmoy often says that although we may have difficulty meditating, we can all sing devotedly, and when we do so, our consciousness can be elevated in exactly the same way as a good meditation.

Sometimes I will have music playing in the background while I meditate. It seems to both satisfy and occupy the mind so it is more comfortable in its silence.

I've included two songs on the next page which are simple and inspiring. These songs were written by Sri Chinmoy. If you are not a musician, perhaps a friend can help you with the melodies. These songs are also availaible on our website, but you have to tolerate me singing them!

> In the spiritual world, next to meditation
> is music, the breath of music.
> Meditation is silence, energising and fulfilling.
> Silence is the eloquent expression
> of the inexpressible.
>
> s.c.

My own gratitude-heart

Text and music
by Sri Chinmoy

November 1987

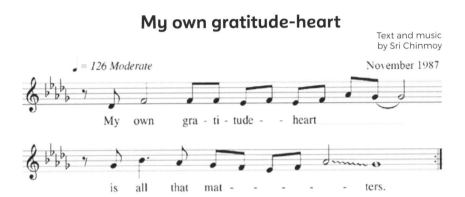

Beauty came to me

Text and music
by Sri Chinmoy

⊙ Spiritual discrimination

Finally, with regard to the mind, start the practice of spiritual discrimination. Decide to live your life with a sense of wisdom.

> The soulful prayer and the music world of a seeker-musician are the same thing. His soulful music is his soulful prayer, and his fruitful meditation is another name for his fruitful music. ❧ s.c.

Ask yourself, "Do I need to have this particular experience? Is it good or necessary for me to do this?" An immediate consequence of this kind of spiritual discrimination will be a simplification of your life. You will become less "cluttered" with unnecessary things—less worries, less tensions—more sweetness and joy.

Meditation for the heart

By all means, practise your meditation for the sake of consciously accessing and developing the heart. Practise this thing called love, selfless love, unconditional love. Cultivate it in the inner domain through your meditation, then practise it in the outer domain in your relationships at work and at home. In addition to love, the heart will present an entire new vantage point—a vantage point that is based on its sense of oneness with others and the world around you. With the establishment of oneness, many of the separativity issues associated with the unillumined side of our being weaken, and finally disappear.

There are three qualities which dominate the heart atmosphere. We are all familiar with the quality of love, but there are two more that represent enhanced and enlarged expressions of love. These are devotion and surrender. Love, devotion and surrender are the three qualities of the heart which represent the essence of the heart experience and must be cultivated in the course of one's spiritual development. I borrow from Sri Chinmoy's *Songs of the Soul* again:

Love, Devotion and Surrender

" *Love is action. Devotion is practice. Surrender is experience.*

Love is realisation. Devotion is revelation. Surrender is manifestation.

Love is the meaning of life. Devotion is the secret of life. Surrender is the Goal of life.

In my love, I see God the Mother. In my devotion, I see God the Father. In my surrender, I see God the Mother and God the Father together in one body.

Love without devotion is absurdity. Devotion without surrender is futility.

Love with devotion was my journey's start. Devotion with surrender is my journey's close.

I love the Supreme because I came from Him. I devote myself to the Supreme because I wish to go back to Him. I surrender myself to the Supreme because He lives in me and I in Him.

(From Songs of the Soul, "Love, Devotion, Surrender")

Exercise / Meditation on Love, Devotion and Surrender

This meditation exercise is another one of my favorites. It combines visualization techniques with something akin to mantra. Of course, begin with your ABC's, assuming the correct posture, inner diligence and commitment.

Please envision in your heart your most favorite flower. (If you have difficulty imagining a flower, place a flower in front of you. Concentrate on it and then close your eyes to see it inside your heart.) See it as clearly as you can (but it is okay if the inner flower changes as you see it inside). Its colours are vivid. Remain still with this flower in your heart for a minute or two.

Now, on each petal of the flower, write the three words: Love, Devotion, Surrender. But do more than just write the word. Each time you write the word "love", imagine that you love God (and remember, you can use any word/concept with which you are comfortable), that you love God unconditionally. When you write the word "devotion", allow yourself to feel a moment's willingness to devote yourself to God. When you write the word "surrender", imagine that your entire being surrenders to the will of the Supreme, that you are a drop falling into and becoming one with the ocean that is God. Do this with each petal in turn—Love, Devotion, Surrender.

Finally, imagine that God is standing right in front of you and with utmost humility, soulfulness and gratitude, offer your heart-flower at the feet of God, or to the Universal Consciousness.

Living a meditative lifestyle

What can we conclude here? We see that meditation is not merely sitting for five or ten minutes in the morning. If you want to reap the rewards of meditation and, if you want to cultivate a holistic sense of peace in your entire existence, then *you have to live a meditative lifestyle.* Your outer life and your inner life are intimately linked. Don't meditate to escape the world, but rather to integrate your inner life and your outer life. In this way, you can begin experiencing more harmony from moment to moment.

Our inner life can bring peace to our outer life and our outer life can encourage our inner life. Sri Chinmoy says that we need both the inner life and the outer life. We need the soul for our inner or spiritual realisation and we need the body for the manifestation of the soul. Extending that into the world, Sri Chinmoy clarifies that the spiritual life is not a life of renunciation, but a life of acceptance. We must accept the outer life with an eye to transforming it.

> "Devotion is a soul-stirring emotion. It dynamically permeates the entire consciousness of the devotee. Devotion is action. This action is always inspired by the devotee's inner being. — s.c.

Spiritual development is indeed a holistic phenomenon. Every day we should eat proper inner food and outer food. Every day we should meditate to nourish our inner life. Every day we should exercise, because that's going to help the body in its transition from being lethargic to being a temple. Every day we should seek some creative outlets to encourage the vital out of its aggression and into its dynamic creativity and service. Every day we should discipline the mind in the direction of right thought and wisdom. Everyday we should exercise the heart by trying to be loving, compassionate and just. These efforts will allow us to become the best human beings we possibly can and, with that sense, tremendous satisfaction will dawn in our lives.

Below, I summarise the things that you might do to bring meditation to your entire life:

1) Upon awakening, wash off the sleep consciousness with a shower and immediately sit at your designated area to meditate. You might include at this time some singing of spiritual songs or listening to spiritual music and chanting.
2) Meditate regularly and punctually.
3) Create a space that is dedicated to your meditation.
4) Read and study inspiring writings for half an hour to an hour a day.
5) Exercise daily, 20 minutes to an hour. Running/walking are particularly good. Consecrate your exercise as part of your spiritual process. In other words, don't just go out for a walk, but begin your walk with a minute of meditation. As you walk, remember why you are doing it—to make the body-temple stronger. Perhaps chant "AUM" or "Supreme" with every step.
6) Listen to inspiring music.
7) Seek out creative and selfless outlets—activities that allow you to serve without thought for self.
8) Take cues from life to remember your spiritual life. Most people wash their hands before eating. How about meditating for a minute before you eat? Or a minute before you drive somewhere?
9) Designate some specific time when you practise japa, chanting or singing.
10) Consider a vegetarian diet, which will definitely help your meditation.

11) Consider eliminating unnecessary or uninspiring activities. For example, I read the newspaper only once a week
because, frankly, it doesn't change that much from day-
to-day!

> "Surrender has the strength to meet
> the Absolute and stay and play with
> Him eternally. God may at times play
> hide-and-seek with man's other divine
> qualities, but never with His devotee's
> genuine surrender. S.C.

Before one meditates, the body, vital and mind are constantly imposing their respective agendas upon us. It is easy to see why we can often feel conflicted. We "know" we should do one thing, "feel" like doing another. On the other hand, maybe we'll just do nothing at all. As a result of regular meditation practice something happens—something that is very, very important. Before meditation, the body, vital and mind sheaths all talk at once. There is no "inner order". And the sum total of these agendas create your sense of self,

The Beginning of Self-Mastery

sometimes clear, sometimes confused, and perhaps even conflicted.

But, when you regularly meditate, the various layers settle down and define themselves and their agendas much more clearly. Each one of these layers has a distinctively different voice, a distinctively different "colour", a distinctively different feeling about it.

To a certain extent, the sense of these different voices is common knowledge. When we experience anger, we'll often say we feel it in the pit of our stomach. It is not a coincidence that the vital is located in that vicinity. When we have a strong heartfelt feeling, we experience it in the centre of our chest where the spiritual heart is located. That's why when people experience this, they often refer to it as being "centred". When we're really in the mind, we can feel ourselves in our heads. Think of how you feel when you just completed paying your bills or filing your taxes!

> **Your self-mastery Is exceedingly powerful. Your God-discovery Is eternally fruitful.**
>
> — s.c.

When you quiet your inner being during your meditation, the different parts of your being and their voices become much more clear. Recognizing the different voices of these inner sheaths is extremely important because *it provides an inner criterion to gauge your life existence.* You'll begin to recognize the heart's response. Over time, its voice becomes clearer and clearer. In the same way, the voice of each sheath will become more evident. Not only do the sheaths themselves become clear, but also the illumined/non–illumined aspects become distinct as well. You will know when your illumined heart speaks. You will know when your unillumined vital speaks. It is based on these clear inner voices that you can gauge your actions and interactions in the world.

Let me emphasise that this criterion is based *not on anything outside* yourself, but only on something *inner.* By following the proper inner voice, you can expedite your progress toward the illumined side of your consciousness.

If an experience in life compels you in the direction of the illumined side of your being, you'll say "yes" to the experience. If, on the other hand, an experience draws you toward the unillumined side of your being, you'll say "no" to that experience, or alternatively, choose to change the experience into something positive.

Suppose you meet and interact with someone and you feel your heart respond. By virtue of this inner criterion, you can put your faith in the encounter. Alternatively, if your response comes from the unillumined vital, you now have a choice. Do you choose to move around it, and then come back to it later when you have developed the inner fortitude to deal with it? Or, do you have the inner fortitude now to lift this interaction into the heart, that is, to change the nature of the interaction?

As a result of this new awareness of the inner layers, you will get a sense that you are becoming a more conscious participant in your own life processing. No longer are you merely a pinball bouncing off life experiences, but you now have an *inner* standard by which you can assess and change your life.

I have already spoken about the purpose of life—to realise God, to realise the highest Truth and to manifest that Truth in your life. But many people don't resonate with "God" language. Instead of God-realisation, you can use the term "self-mastery". The development of an inner standard by which you judge your life's interactions is the dawning of self-mastery.

You will quickly discover that you do many things because you have been conditioned by your surroundings to do them! We have all been "advertised", "parent-ised", "friend-ised", "social-ised". Indeed, much of this conditioning can be good. But now, based on the development of an inner criterion, you will act because you know in your heart that it is the right thing to do.

> "Prepare yourself for self-mastery, since God has already prepared you for self-discovery. — s.c.

Now, in spite of developing this inner criterion, sometimes you will make the wrong choice. Our conditioning may have led to many bad habits. But, at least now the criterion is clear. When life activity motivates you "heartward" you will try to say "Yes," and when it doesn't, then you will try to say "No."

A moment to clarify "the heart"

Unfortunately, "feeling something in your heart" are words too often used in romantic cliché. It is *not* the emotional feeling that rises from the gut. This kind of emotion comes from the vital and is very different from the heart's emotion.

Vital emotions come with an intensity or urgency. They have to be satisfied in a particular way. Otherwise, dissatisfaction looms large. Emotions from the heart are more like revelations. They have a sense of revelatory joy about them. When you experience the heart's emotions, it feels as though something joyful has been revealed to you—something that you always knew was there, but was simply hidden from sight.

Take time to allow your meditation to redefine what your spiritual heart really is. You will discover that the heart is a living reality quite different from anything romantic.

A healthy inner disassociation

Spiritual progress is often said to be a peeling away of that which is *not* you, to discover that which is *truly* you. Much of what is *not* you is like the crust that surrounds the snowball, and that crust coincides well with the unillumined "body-vital-mind" sheaths.

Who you are is something else besides the mind's thoughts, the vital's base feelings and the body's tendency toward lethargy.

You are not necessarily "what you think" yourself to be! This recognition creates a healthy disassociation which can prove to be quite liberating. Allow me to demonstrate with a story.

I have two dear friends, both of whom struggled with a similar physical malady. One of these friends is Ashrita Furman. Ashrita has the unique world record of holding the most world records in the Guinness Book of World Records. Among the records he now holds or has held: somersaulting distance; jumping rope for 24 hours; pogo-sticking up Mt. Fuji; walking while balancing a milk bottle on his head; walking while hula hooping and many, many more.

Here is Ashrita during a record attempt for walking with a milk bottle balanced on his head!

Breaking world records has become his own personal expression of spiritual transcendence-progress, and he always does these things with a tremendous sense of joy and inspiration. He is someone of seemingly indefatigable energy and strength who is filled with life energy.

A few years back, after pogo-sticking in the Amazon River (Yes, you read correctly. He called it "aqua-pogo"!), he unfortunately contracted a parasitic illness which affected his liver. Whenever this condition would flare up, one of the symptoms was that his mental state would become very dark. I remember him describing it to me this way (and this is the important part so read it carefully!): "When this liver thing flares up, my thoughts become very dark, very depressed, and I have to fight with my mind like crazy."

On to friend number two who had a similar problem (and this should make the point clear). Whenever his condition flares up, he says, "I get so depressed; it's so dark. I can't find a way out." Notice the subtle but important difference in the language. In Ashrita's case, *his thoughts and mind are different from who he is*, while in friend two's case, as goes his mind, so goes he.

As we witness ourselves along with the interaction of the various sheaths, we are free to re-identify ourselves with the innermost part of our being. Indeed, I am NOT what I think. I am NOT the mind's limitations. I am NOT the vital's anger. I am NOT the body's lethargy.

Our work in life becomes inner work. Certainly I am responsible to act in the world, but while doing so, I must inject the body with life energy, I must purify the vital, I must illumine the mind, I must cultivate the heart, I must honour the voice of the soul.

A glimpse of the spiritual Teacher

Although I dedicate an entire chapter later in this book to the role of the spiritual Teacher, at this point I want to mention that having a spiritual Teacher plays an especially important role with regard to learning to identify the various inner voices.

The Guru can kindle the lamp in you. When? Only after you have brought him the wick and the oil. — s.c.

Before we begin meditating, each of the sheaths will express its agenda and we are not yet in a position to recognize just what is coming from where. As we meditate, as I mentioned, the various sheaths become more distinct, but this process does not happen overnight. Furthermore, the voice of the heart is easily drowned out by the voices of the unillumined parts of our being.

It does not take a whole lot of humility to admit that in the beginning we don't have the tools to recognize, for example, what is heart versus what is vital. A genuine Teacher, however, can clearly see these things and reinforce them for you. He can easily affirm to you what the heart's voice is saying, and in this way, help you recognize its subtleties.

And of course, life is not all black and white. We may go through periods in our lives and in our meditations when everything is gray. At these times, a Teacher can guide the seeker through the darker periods. The Teacher simply holds onto the seeker's heart-hand and guides him to a place where he can see more clearly.

> **"** If you want to change your life, then do not waste your time going here and there. Go to the right person: your illumining soul. ✿ S.C.

Eggs and onions

A true story. God bless my father. He was, without a doubt, the greatest scrambled egg-maker in the world. He was very proud of his scrambled eggs. No matter what time of day I would arrive at my parent's New York home on my visits from Chicago, I would be received with a hug and a "Lemme make you some scrambled eggs." My father's scrambled eggs were nothing short of beautiful. Sometimes he would make them straight, sometimes with a little fried onions, perfectly glazed. Every short order cook who works for me gets this story, along with the instructions, "Whenever you make eggs, invoke my father's soul. Imagine him standing there behind you, watching. Make them beautiful."

What has this to do with meditation? Well, very little actually save for the fact that it makes a nice segue to this little life exercise.

Exercise / **Eggs and onions**

This little exercise serves to help you take responsibility for your own world from the inside-out! Imagine that you yourself live within a large egg. It is just large enough to accommodate you. Furthermore, this egg is totally transparent so others can't see it, but you know it's there.

Your job, for one hour, is to make everything inside this egg perfect. Let every bit of consciousness-energy-emotion that you exude in this shell be free of doubt, insecurity, critical thought, anger, jealousy. Your task is to fill this space with nothing but good will, joy and all of its related feelings.

At the same time, allow no one else's negative experiences to penetrate the egg. This is your space to keep clean and perfect.

Although I frame this little exercise light heartedly, do not overlook its importance. This is about changing yourself, your reaction pattern and your behaviour in the world. It may sound easy to do, but see for how long you can do it. With continued practice, increase the amount of time and the size of the egg for which you are responsible.

> To change your outer life
> What you need is determination-strength.
> To change your inner life
> What you need is patience-length.
>
> S.C.

To recap, first of all, through meditation we're developing an inner criterion to gauge the value of our life experience. Secondly, we've learned that the inner life and the outer life are entwined and we should consider meditation not just as an activity, but as a lifestyle.

It's important to under-stand that as the quality of one's meditation improves, the inner movement that takes place becomes more active. To appreciate this, let's look at how much of the soul's light actually inundates each sheath.

Spiritual Transformation

Remember that I first intro-duced the heart as the "place" to meditate because the animating element, the soul, abides in the heart room. And by virtue of this intimacy, the heart is essentially completely inundated with the soul's light. This is why the words "heart" and "soul" are often used interchangeably but they are, in fact, two different things.

With each successive sheath, less of the soul's light penetrates—less of the soul's light gets into the mind, even less of the soul's light enters into the vital, and only dribbles of it enter into the physical in a normal everyday life.

Your meditation is not intended to be merely a passive process. As with playing a musical instrument, with regular practice the quality of your meditation improves. As you improve in your meditation, you will not only access the heart, but also bring the light of the soul from the heart to the mind and, in so doing, consciously *transform* the nature of the mind from the separating, criticising, analytical doubting mind to the intuitive, discriminatory, visionary mind. You'll bring the inner light to the vital and *transform* the nature of the vital from being aggressive to being dynamic and creative. You'll bring light to the body and *transform* the nature of the body. This process is ongoing, from moment to moment—a process of slow but steady transcendence in every aspect of your life.

> **There is no difference between human transformation and divine Perfection.** — S.C.

In the spiritual process, nothing is destroyed. You will come to recognize many right things about your nature which you will try to encourage, and also some wrong things about your nature that need correction. This correction process is not a matter of excising the wrong, but rather a matter of transforming it by illumining it.

Consider a room with no light in it. Of course, it may be very difficult to function in such a room. Does this mean that the room is inherently bad or useless? No! All that we need to do is to simply turn the light on! Similarly, there may be parts of our nature which are quite unillumined. The solution is not to cut them out, but simply to bring light in. In so doing, we transform our nature from darkness to light, to brighter light, to brightest light.

Please note that spiritual *progress* is equivalent to gradual *"transformation/transcendence"*. The joy in spiritual processing does not come from absolute success, but rather, from our continual progress. Indeed, progress itself may be made of small steps of both success and failure. We must not be quick to judge our own progress in terms of a day or a week or a month. Remember the infant who is attempting to walk. He tries and flops down, and tries and flops down again and tries and flops down once more. Over time and after much effort, he succeeds. But that success has been built on hundreds of failed attempts.

I doubt that at any time does the child think, "I can't do this." (Perhaps self-doubt and defeat are something that we learn as we grow older.)

> " No failure, no failure.
> Failure is the shadow of success.
> No failure, no failure.
> Failure is the changing body of success.
> No failure, no failure.
> Failure is the fast approaching train
> of the greatest success. ❧ s.c.

In exactly the same manner as with the infant, we are trying to crawl, walk and run in the spiritual life. Joy is born when we witness our own progress. There may be times when we have experiences of failure and success. This is to be expected, but trust that *no sincere effort will remain unfruitful.*

Transcendence is part and parcel of any genuine spiritual processing. Transcendence means making today's achievement the starting point for tomorrow's new goal. If this week we ran a mile a day, then next week let us try to run one and a half or two miles. Each seeker, having his/her own inner disposition, may choose a different pace, but transcendence should be present in all aspects of life. If today, we have achieved a drop's worth of peace, then tomorrow let us try to cultivate two drops, then three drops, a small pond of peace, a lake, an ocean.

The transformation of sexual energy

Historically, serious spiritual seeking is associated with a disciplining of sexual expression. For example, priests and monks take a vow of celibacy as part of their training. And it is indeed true that the achievement of higher states of consciousness is associated with a transformation in sexual energy. This process often frightens the Western seeker for two reasons:

1) We make a tremendous investment in our sexual identities. As a result, disciplining ourselves sexually is equated with "giving up" something, and
2) The process is completely misunderstood. In fact, nothing is being given up—only how it is being expressed is being changed, and in fact, intensified!

Let's dialog a bit:

Why do we partner at all? I believe the ultimate reason is that there is the hope that partnering will make us more whole.

Consider what it is about someone that attracts you to him/her. Certainly, the overriding hope is for a shared love. We want to love and equally important, we want to be loved. Typically, other qualities must also be present when considering a suitable partner, among them strength of character, beauty, security, a sense of oneness, to name a few. One might even admit to seeking something everlasting, "Will you be mine forever?"

Now, if the qualities are not there, we don't find the person attractive or, depending on how "needy" we are, we may be willing to settle for a not-so-perfect mate. But clearly, if the qualities are absent, then the person is not suitable. What can we conclude? We find someone attractive because they embody to some extent qualities that we need to fulfil ourselves! It's the qualities that we want!

Look carefully at these qualities. Are they not qualities which are found on the original lists we made way back when asked, "What qualities give your life meaning?" (see page 28). To me, it seems clear that the mating game is an attempt to fulfil a spiritual need.

The spiritual process is about becoming whole by virtue of one's communion with one's higher self. The quest for love, oneness, beauty, something eternal, union, are all still present. In fact, they are intensified—much, much intensified. What is different is how this need is fulfilled. In the spiritual life, one seeks to fulfil these things inwardly, whereas in the typical human mating process, one seeks these things in someone else who is seeking them back! I refer to human love as reciprocal-need-fulfilment with someone who meets, to some extent, your inner/outer requirements. As I mentioned earlier, Swami Vivekananda was more direct in referring to human love as "marketing".

Human love is "need" based, and therefore subject to the laws of all desire, that is, it is bound to change. Human love is give and take. We offer something, we expect something back—a smile, an acknowledgment, a "thank you" of some sort.

Divine love is something different. Divine love is unconditional and self-fulfilling—to offer it is to become overwhelmed with the sense of love itself.

> "The difference between human love and divine love is very simple:
> Human love desperately needs.
> Divine love abundantly feeds.
> — s.c.

Does it not make sense to learn the essence of love before one goes about offering it to others? Human sexuality and all of its emotions are situated in the unillumined vital. Spiritual love is founded in the illumined heart. The shift in sexual expression is not at all a negation of the need for love. Quite the contrary. It reflects a conscious decision to choose the unconditional love of the illumined heart over the limited love of the unillumined vital.

Some authorities suggest that sexual energy and spiritual energy are related, that they are actually the same force only channeled through different energy centres. So in transforming sexual expression, one is not giving up anything. Instead, the process is one of channeling that same energy up through higher spiritual centres. You still seek love, union and oneness, but the source from which you seek it is your own soul. The task becomes not merely to love someone or something, but to be all-loving.

"But I can't do that!"

Oh, no? I believe this perception is more a reflection of one's investment in one's sexuality than anything else. I want to share another story with you, but allow me to preface it by saying that it is not my intention to demean the issue of sexual transcendence/transformation at all, but simply to make a point.

I am extremely, extremely close with my younger brother, Billy. Now, when he was a youngster, oh, about five or six years of age, his constant companion was his "tickle-shirt". You would swear that this tickle-shirt was physically attached to him. The tickle-shirt was a very thin, sleeveless style undershirt that he would carry in his right hand, fist clenched, thumb extended so as to fit comfortably in his mouth (the thumb, not the tickle-shirt). Furthermore, it had to be dirty. Whenever my mother washed it, he would immediately go out to the nearest car and wipe the dirt off a hubcap to make it appropriately dirty.

Now, if I or anyone were to approach him at this age and suggest that in just a few years he would be giving up that tickle-shirt, you can imagine his reaction. In my more mischievous "older brother" moments, when I attempted to dislodge the tickle-shirt, he would always hold onto it more tightly and respond with either a nasty grunt or release an "unholy" scream from some other world, depending on his mood. This was always followed by a "Sandy, leave your brother alone," coming from my mother elsewhere in the house.

> **Be universal in your love. You will see the universe to be the picture of your own being.**
>
> — s.c.

But of course, just a few years later he did give up that tickle-shirt. And now, if I ever bring it up, all hell breaks loose again. Should he ever read this section, oh God!

I'm guessing my point is obvious. My brother gradually grew out of his need for his tickle-shirt, but this surrender was inconceivable only a few years previous.

Often as adults, we react the same way to the possibility of transforming our sexual expression. For many individuals, it's "just not possible" and the mere suggestion makes us hold onto it more tightly. But as we go through more and more inner experiences, our position on it changes. It actually becomes less essential because we find something more desirable to replace it—union with the inner-self.

I'd like you to begin this chapter by pausing to repeat the gratitude meditation. This was the second exercise you performed. You'll find this exercise on page 50. Why this is important will become clear in a bit.

(A pause while you meditate...)

I hope by now you have a sense of what meditation is and how it is going to affect your own inner environment. The body, vital, mind and heart can be thought of as the immediate external environment of the soul. How the soul affects this immediate environment I call "phase one" transformation.

But there is another phase which I refer to as "phase two" transformation, which is you interacting with your world. This is when things typically become a little more challenging. Most people find it fairly easy to meditate by themselves or with a group of like-hearted people. That's like running

Problems and Adversities

with the wind at your back! However, maintaining your inner poise or your inner joy in outer circumstances, which are more often than not out of your control, can be much more difficult.

The key to succeeding (or perhaps making progress would be the preferred description!) is to remember and constantly re-identify with your ever-present inner occupation. You are not merely an executive, secretary, pharmacist, nurse or whatever. This is a label which has only temporary meaning. This outer definition, and its concomitant script, may change from hour to hour. Instead, declare to yourself that your occupation is to progress forward on the consciousness line. Every day your responsibility is to nurture peace, joy and love inside yourself. Instead of using the term nurturing, the term "seeking" is often used. You are a seeker. (Now, I am not suggesting that when you introduce yourself to someone you say, "I'm a seeker." You'll get a lot of strange looks. This is your private inner occupation.)

> May a gratitude-flower be found
> in each heartbeat of mine.
>
> s.c.

Two life-tasks

Progressing forward on the consciousness line in its simplest form translates into doing only two tasks:

1) Taking what is bad about you (a weakness) and making it good (a strength) [→ Transformation], and
2) Taking what is good about you and making it even better. [→ Transcendence].

Continually applying yourself to these efforts makes for the possibility of constant progress.

If we can acknowledge these two tasks, then we can immediately recognize the merit in knowing what is good about our nature and knowing what is bad about our nature. It is only by first knowing our strengths and weaknesses that we can go about the process of illumining and transcending them.

Of course, our meditation is an invaluable tool in this process. It is true that proper meditation will bring light forward into the being and with that may come many illumining experiences. But it is also true that with the increase in light will come an increased awareness of the weaknesses in our nature. In fact, many people comment that after meditating for a few months or a year they are aware of many more imperfections in their nature. I often hear comments such as, "Since meditating I'm happier, but I sometimes feel that I've become a worse human being!" Of course, this is not the case. These weaknesses were always present in their nature, but were insidious. By shining light on the inner nature, meditation simply revealed them so that ultimately they can be illumined.

> None can deny the fact that every step of progress which the world has made has come from both the smiles of prosperity and the tears of adversity. — S.C.

Again, it is important that one not be overly consumed by their so-called weaknesses. Inner diligence and wisdom are necessary here. Recall what I said earlier, that these weaknesses are merely places where there is less light. It is one thing to acknowledge a weakness and quite another to obsess over and identify with that weakness. We must acknowledge a weakness only so far as it is a necessary first step to illumine it. You might simply consider your collective weaknesses as determining your inner life assignment list. Conquer your anger with oneness-patience, illumine your fear with courage and so on and so forth.

As soon as we adopt this attitude toward our weaknesses, then we will see that the world serves as a wonderful theater which schools us in our life progress.

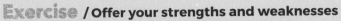

Exercise / **Offer your strengths and weaknesses**

On one of our Christmas vacations, Sri Chinmoy offered a simple meditation exercise. You can include it as part of a larger meditation, or it may stand on its own. It is quite simple. Consider a weakness in your nature and envision it as a flower. Soulfully offer this flower to the Supreme. Repeat this for seven weaknesses, that is, envision seven weaknesses as flowers and offer each flower to the Supreme. In the exact same way, envision three strengths as flowers, and offer those to the Supreme. Guru said, "In this way, you will see your weaknesses gradually disappear and your strengths come to the fore."

Learning our life's lessons

The world serves as a wonderful vehicle, a teacher if you will, to expose us to our own weaknesses and to reveal to us our strengths. Allow me to explain this with a simple story. A friend of mine was a theater major at Northwestern University. He was in a master's program, his specialty being set design. Subsequent to a performance, it was his task to save the backdrop. The way he described it, the canvas backdrop was about 60 feet wide and 15 feet tall with multiple supporting boards in the framework. It was stapled every three inches, so you might imagine how many staples he had to remove.

As he was performing his task, two of his students (in the master's program you have students) came and offered their assistance, which he gladly accepted. After about half an hour, the two students had enough of staple removing. One of them approached him saying, "I don't know how you can do this. I don't want to see another staple in my life. I don't know how you can keep removing staples like this." To which he responded, "Oh, I'm not removing staples. I'm practising my patience!"

We might all understand getting frustrated at such a task. After all, we've got more important things to do than the task at hand, don't we?! Consider the traffic jam experience. You're sitting on the highway, inhaling fumes, and you're getting angry. Ask yourself, "What value is there in my anger? Will it get me to my destination any faster?" More importantly, "Will it get me to my destination any happier?"

> "I pray to God to transform my life into one long effort, fearless and egoless, so that I can derive the most fulfilling achievements from the most unpromising situations.
>
> — S.C.

Every year 200 to 300 of Sri Chinmoy's students run a major marathon. There are many excellent runners in the Sri Chinmoy Centres. As I mentioned earlier, I am not one of them, but I've run a marathon on many occasions. How I approach the marathon is what compels me to succeed. True, outwardly I am running, but inwardly, I am practising determination and staying in a joyful consciousness for a few hours. When I start a marathon, I say to myself, "Look, I'm determined to do this. For four to five hours I'm going to be out there keeping my legs moving. For four to five hours I'm going to stay happy." If either of these fail me, then it's time for me to stop.

Additionally, during the marathon itself, I perform inner exercises to support my consciousness. For example, at every mile marker, for two minutes I offer gratitude to the Supreme for having given me the capacity to run, and for allowing me to complete another mile.

Quite clearly, ultimately everything can translate into some kind of inner exercise. Inner qualities are like muscles, and we can strengthen them by exercising them. Now, I'm not suggesting to you that every time you trip over a crack you ask yourself, "Oh what does that mean? How does this translate into some inner dimension?" No. But you will witness certain situations that regularly challenge you or cause you difficulty. When these situations present themselves as negative obstacles, what have you got? PROBLEMS! Yes, problems, and we've all got them.

Problems, problems, problems

Why does something present itself as a problem to us? *Something becomes a problem for us not because it exists, but because that something, whatever it is, disrupts our inner harmony.* Two people can walk through the exact same life circumstance. One person can walk through with a certain degree of poise and dignity, while the second person becomes completely frazzled and stressed out by it. As part of any class, I ask people why they come to the class. In university settings, almost always, there is one person on one side of the room who says, "Well, next week is finals and I'm completely freaking out. I thought this might help," while on the other side of the room, "Well, next week is finals. I've got nothing else to do, so I figured I'd come by."

Of course, part of this particular difference in attitude may be due to outer preparation, but I suspect you get the point. These two people are both approaching the same life experience, but one has a tremendous loss of poise, while the other one is perfectly calm. I think we all know of circumstances like this. We know someone who seems to have better coping skills and wonder how they deal with things so calmly, while we're having a hard time. In other circumstances, perhaps these roles might reverse, that is, you can cope while the next person can't.

Why? It bears repeating. *Something becomes a problem for us simply because it disrupts our inner harmony.* Otherwise, it's not a problem—it's just something to do. Therefore, it behooves us to develop the necessary inner assets to be able to cope with life. We are not doomed to be victims in life. No! The more you develop inner strength, the more inner assets you have. The more inner assets you have, the more coping capability you have, and things simply won't bother you. In fact, this increased ability to cope, this calm in the storm is often the first tangible sign that your meditation is working. In time, when problems confront us, it will not be a matter of how we cope, but how we resolve!

> " A problem exists only in our own consciousness. The same external situation becomes a problem for me but not for you. Why? Because it disturbs some element of my inner harmony, while yours is left untouched. ❧ s.c.

In general, problems can be categorised into two major types:

1) **Situational**, that is, problems that seem to come from outside of us—an unhealthy work situation or friendship.
2) **Personal**, that is, problems that have as their causation an inner flaw. We may have a tendency towards anger, jealousy, insecurity or fear. These problems may arise in response to a situation, but clearly stem from an inner weakness. For example, one can be sitting in the privacy of one's own room and become fearful just pondering the next day's agenda.

In either case, the solution has to do with reestablishing our inner poise, which then transforms the situation out of the problem domain and into the opportunity domain. There are a number of methods to do this, but all these methods have to do with changing how we respond to certain stimuli or cues.

> There is no other way to spiritual success than to sit at the feet of Patience, trusting to her lords, Time and Progress. ❧ s.c.

The meditative life, as a life of discipline, is often referred to as a life of self-mastery. What this means is that we have to take hold of our inner responses and change them. We are under no obligation to feel angry, jealous or insecure. To a certain extent, in some perverse ways, we enjoy these feelings because at least they add a flare of drama to our lives. It is a sort of reverse ego. We tend to feel that there is a certain merit in having more problems than the next person—our life is tougher, we deserve more sympathy and at the same time, more tolerance for our shortcomings. This is an insult to our human potential. True, as a human beings, we have our flaws. But instead of viewing ourselves as helpless victims of these flaws, let us become heroes by conquering these flaws and transforming them into strengths.

Don't look back

This approach to solving our life problems is in stark contrast to many contemporary schools of psychotherapy, which encourage individuals to "get into" their angers (or other negative qualities) and express them in order to be released from them. Furthermore, tremendous investment is often made looking backwards in time to discover why an individual suffers from these things in the first place. In general, I am not a proponent of either of these two methodologies. (To all the psychotherapists out there who may be reading this, I beg your forgiveness!)

You see, who you are right now at this very moment is the product and summation of everything that came before you. True, looking back in time may give you an explanation as to why you behave in a certain way, *but it does not give you the tools to relinquish the behaviour or transform it into something positive.* "I'm insecure because my father used to berate me all the time as a child." So?! What are you going to do to transform this weakness?

It is you, in your present-day-now version, who is solely responsible for your transformation. And certainly, the easiest and most effective way to be freed from the negative impact of any quality is not to experience it in the first place.

Allow me to confess quite frankly, when I feel anger—no matter how justified the anger may seem—it is I who suffer with it. I am closed up and suffocating under its influence. So let me consciously choose to respond in a different way, a way that is more productive. I do not see any merit in "getting into my anger" and letting the person to whom this anger is directed "have it". In no way, shape or form am I suggesting that justice should not operate. I am suggesting, however, that I am the one who is responsible for how I react and feel, not someone else.

> As soon as you have conquered a difficulty, you will find that it repeats itself on a higher and subtler level. It is the same essential weakness in yourself which you are made to face in a more refined form. ✍ s.c.

Alas, the storyteller in me is once more coming to the fore. In chiropractic, there is an actual syndrome known as "rear wallet syndrome". Some individuals experience back instability and pain due to carrying a large wallet in a rear pocket. This effectively introduces a torque on the pelvis whenever one sits, which can then cause back pain. As a general rule in my office, I would encourage patients to move their wallets to a front pocket to avoid this syndrome.

Often, while explaining the syndrome, I would remove their wallet and place it in my own pocket! "I will take care of your wallet for you," I would tell them. Of course, this was a joke and I would return the wallet before they left the office.

Well, on one fateful day, I forgot to give a patient back his wallet before he left the office. When I realised this, I called him at home and work, leaving messages of apology wherever I could. I made a mistake and tried as best I could to rectify the problem.

He called my office that evening and he was furious—I mean livid. I apologised as profoundly and genuinely as I could, empathised with his situation, offered him everything from free treatments to going to his home to return his wallet. Nothing I could say appeased him. I apologised "from the depth of my heart" at least a half-dozen times, but each time I was greeted with, "I need you to know how angry I am." (By the way, this was precisely what his therapist prescribed for him to manage his anger.) When I realised there was nothing more that I could do or say, and no amount of apology would work, I suggested, "Well, at this point, I'd say you need to work on that anger!" Of course, this was not what he wanted to hear.

> Where forgiveness is in very short supply, Peace will not offer its visible appearance.
>
> S.C.

He retrieved his wallet the next day, and I did not see him again. Three years later, after I left chiropractic and opened a restaurant, this same fellow happened to come in to eat. Seeing me, he approached me and asked if I remembered him and the wallet incident, which I acknowledged. Then he added (and this is the kicker), "Well, now that I've seen what you've done here in the restaurant, I want you to know that I've decided to forgive you!" I thanked him. Privately I felt sad and a bit sorry for him. Can you imagine carrying three years of anger? Who suffered from this? I suspect that there were other unforgiven angers that he must have carried. How could this help make him a happier person? It is my belief that carrying all the misgivings of yesteryears only serves to make one inwardly heavy in the present.

The situational problem

Let us now look more closely at the situational problem. Allow me to invent a little scenario which is not terribly untypical:

You are scheduled to arrive at work at 8 a.m. and, in fact, you arrive 15 minutes early. Right on time, so you think. As if on cue, your boss comes in screaming at the top of his lungs, "Where have you been? I've been here waiting since 7 a.m." Now, you know you are correct. Your boss is terribly angry, unjustifiably so, but angry none the less. Here is a perfect time to respond back in anger, should you choose to do so. Imagine that anger just rising to the surface like steaming volcanic lava ready to explode, completely out of control.

Now, obviously, because you are just reading about this hypothetical situation and not actually in it, you are in a better position to analyze a response. On the one hand, you may be able to justify your anger because, after all, you're in the right. On the other hand, it is clear that anger serves no purpose in this situation. I am not in any way implying that justice should not operate, but anger will not expedite that.

Yet the anger is there and is out of control, so how do you change that response?

⊙ Separation: The essential flaw

The essential flaw in situational problems is lack of oneness—separation. Situational problems occur because the participants allow their consciousness to shift to the left on the consciousness continuum in the direction of separation.

Sri Chinmoy is fond of using his own hands as an analogy. I'll borrow from him once again. I have a right hand and I have a left hand. I happen to be extremely right-handed. It does all the work. If I ever lost it, I would probably starve to death because I would have difficulty getting food into my mouth. (On second thought, I'm sure I'd eventually find a way!)

Now, if this was a life circumstance, say a work situation where my hands represented individuals, my right hand may complain about the left hand, "Hey, I'm doing all the work over here. This left hand over there does nothing. Yet it's getting as much food as I am." Eventually what happens? We have jealousy, we have anger, we have hate. My right hand might become indignant with my left, "Hey ... get your act together, would you please? What's your story?" My left hand might respond, "I'm doing the best I can!" My hands would be in conflict. This is not untypical in outer circumstances.

But, of course, this conflict never takes place between my two hands. Why? Because my two hands recognize that they are part and parcel of the same body. My right hand recognizes that my left hand is part of its own existence.

Here is the key to resolving outer situational problems. Somehow, the response to those life cues which manage to press

> Oneness with the past is our oneness with frustration-night. Oneness with the present is our oneness with hesitation-night. Oneness with the fast-approaching tomorrow is our oneness with God-preparation for a new dawn.
>
> — S.C.

our buttons *must change to reestablish oneness.* And, the responsibility for that may be up to you and you alone, because the other person may not have this understanding at all.

So how does one reestablish this oneness? Indeed, this is one of the great challenges in life. But again, should one master this, it is a most powerful tool. Recognize here and now that we share a common consciousness, a common inner ocean, if you will. And, by changing your own consciousness, you can have an effect on the consciousness of those around you. When you can address life in this way, you're now taking your inner life to the outer world. You're saying, "How can I change the circumstance to uplift the consciousness? Do I have to change me or do I have to change our shared waters? How can I bring joy to this circumstance?" In this particular instance the question is, "How can I reestablish oneness?"

I suspect the answer will surprise you, so let us step back a moment and evaluate.

First, let us assume that we have the humility to admit that anger is an inner response flaw. Why should we have it in the first place? Who needs it or wants it?

Secondly, let us recall that to be aware of one's flaws is a good thing because it is the first step in ultimately transcending them.

Lastly, here is a situation which has exposed us to our weakness. In other words, here is an outer situation which has the very *beneficial* effect of demonstrating an inner weakness in our nature.

> " Only a heart of gratitude and a life of surrender can offer the seeker peace, abundant peace. ⚘ s.c.

All things considered then, what should our proper response be?

Gratitude. (This is why I asked you to perform the gratitude meditation again at the beginning of this chapter.) Yes, you read correctly—gratitude. Think about it a moment. Here is a situation which exposes an inner flaw. That's important information. We should be grateful for having experienced it.

Now, in our hypothetical situation, I am not suggesting that you go over to your boss and say, "Hey thanks. You really got me mad." No! This is an inner exercise and is the beginning of changing your cueing-response pattern. What did we learn about gratitude when we did the meditation exercise? Gratitude creates and embodies joy, love and oneness. *Oneness* is the operative word. In establishing oneness, you calm the shared waters. You respond from a position of poise and dignity, which is always healthier than responding from a posture of anger.

> "If gratitude is there, then inside gratitude you will find power, love, peace and all the divine qualities because gratitude means oneness.
>
> — S.C.

Nor am I suggesting that justice should not operate. Oneness says, "Let us find a solution," as opposed to anger saying "Here's what's wrong with you, buddy." How different these are. The solution may require establishing yourself as an example to the next person—my right hand may choose to train my left hand. Sometimes, it may be a matter of expressing sincere humility in a circumstance. Humility has the power to absorb all the buffets of life.

A beautiful spiritual metaphor is the example of the tree. In a storm it offers protection. When it is laden with fruit, its boughs bend to offer themselves. Even if it is cut down, it offers its stump as a seat. In sincere humility, you lose absolutely nothing. You only gain from extending yourself beyond the limitations that other people may impose upon you.

I often joke that humility is a word that might soon disappear from the dictionary. How sad, because sincere humility is such a beautiful and powerful quality.

Here is the beginning of true reconditioning of your inner environment and changing your outer response patterns, and in this process, gratitude is a wonderful, wonderful, wonderful tool. Whenever you're feeling angry, whenever you're feeling jealous, whenever you're feeling miserable about some outer circumstance, try the gratitude meditation. What you're doing here is exercising your inner muscles. Qualities such as determination, patience, tolerance and forgiveness (and all qualities which we would like other people to offer to us) are like inner muscles that you can strengthen in your outer life by using them.

My Humility

God is my Superior, my only Superior. I am humble to Him. This is my supreme duty. God's children are my equals. I am humble to them. This is my greatest necessity. Pride is my inferior. I am humble to pride. This is my surest safety.

My humility is not self-denial. My humility in silence affirms what I truly have in my world without and what I surely am in my world within.

My humility is not the abstinence from self-love. I love myself. I really do. I love myself because in me the highest Divinity proudly breathes.

Self-conceit tells me that I can easily destroy the world. Self-exploit tells me that the world is at my feet. My humility tells me that I have neither the capacity nor the desire to destroy the world. My humility tells me that the world and I do have the real capacity and the sincere desire to cry for perfect perfection. My humility further tells me that the world is not at my feet, far from it. I carry the world devotedly towards its self-realisation. The world carries me lovingly and openly towards my self-manifestation. When I am all humility, I neither underestimate

nor overestimate my life. What I do is to judge my life exactly,
the way my Lord Supreme judges my life.

  My soul's owner is Divinity. My heart's owner is sincerity.
My mind's owner is clarity. My vital's owner is capacity. My
body's owner is purity.

(From Songs of the Soul, "My Humility")

Our task then is to cultivate these qualities in our meditation, and use them in our outer existence. Of course, each person will have their own set of particular needs. In this way, slowly and steadily, we become stronger and stronger individuals enabling us to interact better and better with the outer world.

The personal problem

The second category of difficulties, personal problems, also requires a change in cueing-response patterns. Again there are tools available to help. With this category of problem, however, understanding the nature of the problem and its solution is perhaps more important because these problems are exclusively ours. Because we are the source of these difficulties, we alone must bear responsibility for their resolution.

In approaching these kinds of problems, it is worth reiterating that the solution comes not from excising the weakness as a surgeon would an inflamed appendix, but rather from transforming the weakness by bringing light into it. Aggression can be transformed into dynamism, fear into courage, doubt into confidence.

Muhammad Ali provided me with a wonderful example of what I am talking about. I had the special opportunity to meet Muhammad on a number of occasions at his home outside Chicago. It is amazing how his persona is just the opposite of that which he portrayed at the height of his boxing career. He was one of the sweetest, gentlest and most humble individuals I have ever met. At any rate, once I sat on his couch thumbing through a coffee table book documenting his boxing career. Page after page showed pictures of him standing over his downed opponents wearing a face of fierce determination and power. I was so impressed with this that I was compelled to ask, "Muhammad, were you ever afraid before a bout?" Can you imagine my surprise when he responded, "Every time. But I used that fear to motivate me." In other words, he transformed the fear into courage.

◎ Use every moment wisely

Typically, when we witness an inner flaw, we respond to it with a wrong feeling or wrong action. Perhaps the most common response is to allow ourselves to become overcome with guilt, remorse and discouragement. This is a great tragedy and spiritually useless. Let's examine this more to understand why I suggest this.

Perhaps the most precious gift we have is time. Life presents us with an infinite number of moments and, with each moment, we can either do the right thing or the wrong thing. Again, allow me to create a little scenario:

Imagine that in three weeks you're going to visit the dentist for triple root canal. You can see it now vividly. You're sitting in the dental chair, mouth filled with cotton, and this masked man (posing as a dentist) approaches you with a six inch needle which he will thrust into your jaw to numb you.

This is all going to happen in three weeks. Can you understand the senselessness of starting to worry about it now? By worrying about some future event, that future event is brought backward in time to the present, destroying the opportunity that the present moment is offering to do the right thing and experience the right happiness.

Conversely, when we feel guilty about some past occurrence, we are simply shifting the time frame, that is, we are bringing some past moment forward to the present, and again, in so doing, we destroy the opportunity that the present moment offers to do the right thing and experience the right happiness. Guilt is resolved when at some moment we forgive ourselves, and thus free ourselves from that past moment. Then we again feel entitled to happiness.

Both of these processes—worrying about the future and feeling guilt about the past—are equally unfruitful. Sri Chinmoy often said that his favorite mantra is "The past is dust." If we should do something wrong or experience something that is outside the boundaries of rightful spiritual experience, the best thing is to *resolve at the very next moment*, with utmost determination, to not make the same mistake again. This resolution must not be frivolous. It should be empowered by proper and sincere meditation. And then the next moment, we should get on with our lives, fully committed to do the right thing and to be the happiest and best person we can be!

Let's face it, it's easy to be content when life is going well and we are playing some productive role in that process. But when things aren't going well and, in particular, when we ourselves

> " I always say, "The past is dust." Once again I repeat, "The past is dust." Why? The past has not given us what we have been striving for. So the past is of no use. It is the present, and the golden future which enters into the present, which make us feel what we are going to be—nay, what we truly are. We are not children of the past, but children of the glorious future. — s.c.

are doing something outside of rightful spiritual action, then it's difficult to be happy. When we do something wrong, we typically impose guilt upon ourselves and with that, self-discouragement and self-doubt. Allow me to phrase this in spiritual terms. It's very easy when things go right to give credit to God or the higher powers. We'll say, "It's not me ... I'm just an instrument." But when things go wrong, suddenly it is all me and we allow ourselves to become separate from the source. Doubt and discouragement enter. We are lesser beings. Indeed, this secondary doubt can be terribly damaging and actually empowers the impact of the original wrong action. Look at how a single thought has the power to strengthen us or weaken us.

> **Each thought is important. Each action is meaningful.**
> s.c.

◉ From thought to action

Thoughts count! The act of doing something wrong always begins by first thinking about doing something wrong. Tracing a thought and how it affects our consciousness is an interesting exercise. Let's revisit that hypothetical work situation when you came to work early but your boss yelled at you. There are five levels of what I call "thought empowerment".

1) You come to work and, after being greeted harshly by your boss, you have a simple thought, something such as, "Gee, he's unusually miserable today," and then you forget about it. You don't think about it again and live the remainder of your day happily. A reactive thought was present but beyond that, it didn't affect you at all. This is the first level.

2) The second level is an extension of the first. After you greet your boss, not only do you think he's miserable,

but you replay his anger throughout your day. Each time you see your boss you bristle a bit, but in between these thoughts and interactions, you're okay. Clearly the experience has a bit of a hold on you, and occasionally robs you of your joy.

3) The third level occurs when the mere sight of your boss ruins your entire day. You not only bristle when you greet him, you obsess over your situation. You fantasise your revenge. Every opportunity for joy is destroyed. This might go on for days or weeks!

4) The fourth level occurs when you act on your thoughts. You go into your boss's office and insult him, his mother, father and dog.

5) The fifth and most damaging level occurs when as a result of your actions you feel guilty, discouraged and doubtful. You think to yourself, "How could I possibly declare myself to be a good person, to be a seeker of truth, when I have done something so wrong!"

Although I used a rather frivolous scenario as my example, the process of going from thought to action generally holds true. With each consecutive level, the degree of damage that is imposed on ourselves gets worse and worse. The fifth level, when we indulge in self-doubt, and its concomitant self-discouragement and self-punishment, is the most toxic. Note that it is quite removed from the original offense. We are "reacting to our reactions".

Many people believe that if they only "think" the wrong thing, then it's okay. I don't agree. Each thought is the beginning of an action.

The converse holds true with regards to right thought. With each right thought, we empower our own goodness. Ultimately, when this right thought manifests itself in good action, we create faith in ourselves.

Once, I approached Sri Chinmoy with a problem that I had been carrying and working on for fifteen years (and still work on today, by the way). Only a few days earlier he had commented that he was pleased with my spiritual progress. Now, three days later I broached him, "Guru, I still have this difficulty in life. I still think the wrong thoughts constantly."

His response was interesting. "Do you remember three days ago when I told you that I was pleased with you?"

"Yes," I said.

He added, "Good. Every time you have this wrong thought remember how pleased I am with you."

> **An unaspiring man has countless duties. All his duties are self-imposed. An aspiring man has only one duty, and that duty is to see the Face of God in himself and in others, and to grow into God's own Face. This is his only God-ordained duty.** — s.c.

I was surprised by his response. You see, this is just the opposite of how I was conditioned to feel all my life. Whenever I would witness these inappropriate thought-actions in my life, I would typically respond with some combination of militaristic-misery theater, ranging from "Oh, God, I've got to fix that. I've got to conquer that," to "I am unworthy, useless and hopeless." With these declarations, I felt that I was putting myself back on the right side of my aspiration. Well, this method doesn't work.

Sri Chinmoy read the surprised (and perhaps perplexed) look on my face. "Yes, every time you have a wrong thought, think a good thought right afterwards. Use the right thought to cure a wrong thought." He added, "When you do something wrong, you run away from light, from your source. You want to hide and, in so doing, you separate yourself from your source. This will only increase the likelihood of you doing the wrong thing again! Instead, you should always include God in your actions, good or bad. In this way, you'll strengthen the good and illumine the bad."

There is a wonderful technique for effecting this shift from darkness to light, called "Ennobling". Ennobling is a very clever method of dissociating ourselves from our inner flaws while at the same time changing our cue-response patterns. Imagine that you suffer from a particular weakness, say, jealousy. Whenever that weakness rears its head, you process it this way: "Isn't it incredible that God (or the Universal Consciousness) has so much faith in me that He's given me a little of the world's jealousy to perfect on His behalf. True, the world is filled with jealousy, but God has faith in me to correct this small part of the world."

> Neither an individual effort nor an individual abnegation can bring about the transformation of your consciousness. This transformation is possible only by the descent of a Higher Light. s.c.

By ennobling, look what we accomplish. Instead of responding negatively to our inner weakness, we have used the weakness to cue us as a reminder toward God. If every time we see a weakness we invoke our higher nature, we will be well on our way to transcending that weakness.

Imagine if every time we did something right and also if every time we did something wrong, we thought of God or gave credit to the higher power. How it would change our lives! We would not allow ourselves to be caught by our own weakness. We would dis-empower the problem. This understanding is the beginning of the changing of our life's cue-response patterns. Remember, and remember again, that to transform a weakness into a strength we must bring light into it.

The responsibilities of life

It often happens that we are challenged by responsibilities. We might feel that our responsibilities are nothing short of burdens. On the other hand, responsibility, or perhaps a better word would be "duty", is part and parcel of life.

Whenever I visited Sri Chinmoy in New York, it was usually an escape from my responsibilities in Chicago. With that escape came more opportunity to meditate and maintain what appeared to be better spiritual discipline. Therefore, I was surprised when Guru commented to me that when I was in Chicago, I made more progress. This was exactly contrary to my perceptions. So I said, "Guru, you know, I don't see it. You say I make more spiritual progress back in Chicago. I don't feel spiritual progress in Chicago. I feel nothing but struggle, nothing but difficulty."

To this he replied, "No, no, no, it's not like that. Think of the weightlifter. The weightlifter lifts weights. Now you can take all the weight off the barbell and the weightlifter says, 'Oh, look how easy it is for me. I can lift the weight so many times.' Now, put weights on the barbell. Immediately he will see it is much more difficult to lift. But, in which way is he developing more strength? When the barbell has weights, of course."

He added, "True, it is more difficult to lift. But at the same time, he is developing more strength. In life, what are your weights? Nothing other than your life's responsibilities. Your life's responsibilities are the weights. So when you go back to Chicago, you assume your life's responsibilities and it is these responsibilities that compel you to develop inner strength."

Sometimes there's a delicate balance between what we deem to be life struggles but in actuality are our true life opportunities. Life is constantly challenging us with the opportunity for transcendence. Once again, we witness that the outer domain and the inner domain are somehow related. The inner and the outer must go hand in hand.

In summary, it can be stated simply that there is only one part of the world over which we can exert rightful responsibility and that is over our own inner environment. Our task is to keep that inner environment clean, joy-filled, poised and powerful. This is the best posture from which to operate in the world.

When I had my first restaurant, many times I had the opportunity to approach Sri Chinmoy with problems. He was always there to give me advice and counsel. One time, after about a half-hour's worth of talking, the final thing he said to me, in the sweetest and most reassuring voice was, "Pradhan, good boy, just be happy and God will solve all your problems."

Now think about it. Is that the deal we seek to cut? No. I think it's just the opposite. We say, "God, just solve all my problems and I'll be happy." Sri Chinmoy's counsel was in just the reverse order! What Sri Chinmoy was suggesting is that when we can create an inner environment of peace, poise, dignity and happiness, that environment allows the higher forces to operate through us so we can better resolve our outer problems.

Take a moment to assess how you feel when you are unhappy. Don't you feel constricted and tight, that nothing is flowing through you at all? If, on the other hand, we keep our inner environment free, the higher aspects of our being are free to operate in us so that we are in a much better position to deal with the world.

Remember, our inner environment is our responsibility. Let us be like a boat in water. If a boat hits stormy waters and there

> " My thought-life
> Is my false happiness.
> My will-life
> Is my true happiness.
> My service-life
> Is my lasting happiness.
> My surrender-life
> Is my everlasting
> happiness.
>
> s.c.

is a hole in the boat which allows the storm to get inside, what happens? The boat fills up with water and has difficulty navigating—it may even sink. But if the boat's hull is intact, and the inside is kept in tune—if the storm is kept out of the boat—then the boat can navigate through the storm. Our task is to keep our inner environment intact, which means being cheerful, joyful, pure, sweet, loving, strong and powerful. Then we can easily navigate through the storms, turmoil and struggles of life.

The following writing, "Be Happy" is again from Sri Chinmoy's *Songs of the Soul.*

Be Happy

Be happy

> *You will grow into God's greatest blessing, His highest pride.*
Be happy
> *Yesterday's world wants you to enjoy its surrendered breath.*
> *Today's world wants you to enjoy its surrendering breath.*
> *Tomorrow's world wants you to enjoy its fulfilling breath.*
Be happy
> *Be happy in the morning with what you have. Be happy in*
> *the evening with what you are.*
Be happy
> *Don't complain. Who complains? The blind beggar in you.*
> *When you complain, you dance in the mire of ignorance-*
> *condition. When you don't complain, all conditions of the*
> *world are at your feet, and God gives you a new name:*
> *aspiration. Aspiration is the supreme wealth in the world of*
> *light and delight.*
Be happy
> *Do you want never to be poor? Then be happy. Do you want*
> *ever to be great? Then be happy.*

Be happy

> *You will get what you like most. You will be what you like best.*

Be happy

> *When you are happy, you and God command each other. God*
> *commands you lovingly. You command God hastily. When*
> *you are unhappy, the hostile forces command you ruthlessly,*
> *doubt commands you openly, bondage commands you*
> *triumphantly and fear commands you unconditionally.*

Be happy

> *God sees in you His aspiring Creation, His transforming*
> *Realisation, His illumining Revelation and His fulfilling*
> *Manifestation.*

Be happy

> *God sees in you another God. God sees you as another God.*
> *God sees you and He as One.*

(From 'Songs of the Soul')

I'm going to return to the consciousness continuum *(the progress line from Finite to Infinite which I showed on page 98)* and superimpose upon it two other progressions that represent different perspectives of human evolution.

From animal to human to Divine

From a phylogenetic perspective, human beings belong to the animal kingdom and, as such, the predominant motivating influence in animals—instinct— still operates in humanity. We might all know people who live their lives based purely, or almost purely, on instinct. Perhaps they are extremely territorial. The simple concept of sharing is not part of their life experience. Social awareness and sensitivities are minimal.

As consciousness evolves, the more philanthropic attitudes begin to play their roles. Values and activities such as

Life Progressions

service, donation of time, family and societal needs become more important than individual satisfaction. Perhaps it might be said that individual satisfaction is found in these activities. This is a shift towards the selflessness side of the consciousness continuum.

As consciousness continues to evolve, the evolution of consciousness becomes the source of satisfaction itself. Nurturing the inner nature becomes the primary focus of the life game.

In overview, the life game can be thought of going from animal to human to divine.

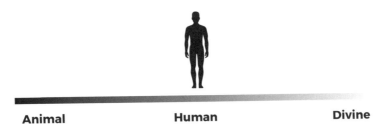

Animal   **Human**   **Divine**

From unconscious to conscious aspiration

A different model can be superimposed on the consciousness continuum based on the forces that drive us. When instinct is the predominant influence, spiritual progress is haphazard. The individual at this stage may not for one moment consider his own spiritual nature. I'm fond of saying that the individual at this stage of development may make more progress between lifetimes than during any lifetime. (Of course, this is based on a belief in reincarnation, and this is another topic altogether!) I refer to this instinctual stage of evolution as the elementary grades of the life school.

At a certain point in the life journey, curiosity dawns in the individual's life. With the simple consideration as to purpose, the potential for spiritual progress is enhanced. I refer to this as the junior high of the life school.

In time, the spiritual aspect of our humanity makes itself felt. The individual at this stage feels some necessity to somehow acknowledge his/her spiritual nature. This is the dawn of aspiration. The individual here may find himself involved in more philanthropic endeavors, social causes and services. I refer to this as the high school of the life school.

> "Time silences the animal in me.
> Time enlightens the human in me.
> Time quickens the divine in me.
>
> ❧ s.c.

Continuing along, an individual reaches a point where the conscious development of their spiritual aspect becomes the primary operating force in their life. He may find himself seeking out a spiritual path and Teacher in order to consciously accelerate spiritual progress. In essence, the individual chooses to be consciously "schooled" in spirituality. I call this period of conscious aspiration the college level of the life school.

Ultimately, your "consciousness-school" places you into a direct relationship with God. At this point, you yourself may appropriately play the role of teacher or guide for your younger brothers and sisters along the road. This is your post-graduate work.

Spiritual progress

instinct   curiosity   aspiration   conscious aspiration

Tolerance

Now, certain things are implicit in these life models. First and foremost is the foundation for tolerance. This life school (or spiritual current or spiritual movement) suggests that we all went through these stages. You never see a professor suggest that an elementary school student is inadequate, because the professor went through that same stage on the way to mastering his own subject. In exactly the same way, we have no right to look at someone and say, "Well, there's a first incarnation if I've ever seen one."

> The Supreme is dearest to us because He is All-Tolerance. But when we go deep within we see that it is not tolerance at all. It is His all-loving Oneness. The Supreme expresses Himself through human imperfection, human limitations and human failure, not on the strength of tolerance, but on the strength of His spontaneous, soulful Concern for His children. — s.c.

In any genuine spiritual path there must be a tremendous sense of tolerance in which the highest, if you will, embraces the lowest. I don't even like to use such terms because it sounds like there's a hierarchy or an arrogance operating, and I don't mean to suggest that. But you can certainly say that a person who is further along the consciousness continuum is in a position to serve, nay, has the responsibility to serve their younger brothers and sisters.

You need not be a college professor to tutor a sixth grader. A high school student may do the job perfectly well. Again, a college professor might have the tools to teach anyone, anywhere along the line. And in fact, this is a large part of our life responsibility. Anyone who is further along the road has the duty to serve as an inspiration for their younger brothers and sisters. This duty should be founded on absolute oneness and never based on superiority.

The law of karma

One might rightfully ask, "Before I actually have a spiritual Teacher, how am I taught?" In fact, you serve as your own teacher by virtue of a very famous spiritual law—the law of karma. The law of karma is beautifully, most simply and perfectly represented by the words of the Christ, "Whatsoever a man soweth, that shall he also reap" or more popularly, "As you sow, so shall you reap." Karma operates like this: when you do something right in life, somehow, someway that right action is positively reinforced in you. Conversely, when you perform wrong action, again, somehow, someway that wrong action is negatively reinforced in you. Sounds simple enough, doesn't it?

> "Service is self-expansion. A sincere seeker serves precisely because he knows that there is and there can be nothing other than service. When he serves aspiring humanity, it is because his inner necessity commands him to serve. —s.c.

Before one enters into the domain of conscious aspiration, karma operates irrevocably. However, after one begins to aspire consciously, then one's karmic influences might be accelerated, or how they are played out in your life might drastically change. This is particularly true when you have adopted a spiritual path and have a spiritual Teacher.

The law of karma is easily stated, but in fact, how it operates is quite complex. Here I must defer to my own teacher and recommend that if you are interested in the process of death, reincarnation and karma, I recommend that you read Sri Chinmoy's *Death and Reincarnation*. I offer this brief excerpt:

Karma

❝Karma is a Sanskrit word meaning action. In the philosophy of the Lord Buddha, the law of karma has its most significant role. In all spiritual paths we must accept the law of karma to some extent. At present, the law of karma is essential because people are still wallowing in the pleasures of ignorance. But when we enter seriously and completely into the sea of spirituality, the law of karma does not always apply.

"As you sow, so you reap"—this is what the law of karma tells us. But who has inspired us to sow? If an undivine force has inspired us, then naturally we shall reap something harmful and destructive. But if we can run towards the highest force, the Supreme, after committing a wrong action, immediately He will come to our rescue. A child does something wrong, but he runs immediately to his father to escape punishment for his deed. He knows that his father can protect him because his father is most powerful.

The past has not given us what we want, so why should we look back? If we think of yesterday as karma, then we will take today as the result. But if today's result is not satisfactory then we must change our outlook. We must take today as karma and tomorrow as the result. Yesterday we were unconscious, undivine, animal; today we have become divinely conscious and aspiring. So naturally, as the result of our karma, tomorrow's golden dawn will be fulfilling.

In the spiritual world, if an aspirant has already made an inner connection with a great spiritual Master, then most of his wrong actions will be nullified by the infinite Grace of the Supreme. At the same time, most of his divine karmic actions will bear fruit sooner than at once. This is because the Master can unite the aspiration of the seeker with the divine Grace, *which is the omnipotent power of the Supreme. If there is no intermediary factor, no spiritual Master, then in spite of doing a good, divine thing, the aspirant will have to wait the full time for the result of his action to take place. Today we sow, and then we have to wait for the harvest. But if the Inner Pilot is consciously aspiring inside us and we are conscious of the Inner Pilot, then we will see that our divine karma will bear fruit immediately.*

(From 'Death and Reincarnation: Eternity's Voyage')

There comes a time in almost every seeker's life when they choose to be consciously schooled in their spiritual processing, and the seeker will adopt a spiritual Teacher and path. Actually, it would be more accurate to say that the Teacher and seeker adopt each other. And, in many regards, the experience and relationship is very much like those that you may have had with other teachers but, in two major ways, it is wonderfully different. First of all, the predominant medium through which lessons are taught is via the silent language of consciousness. Secondly, your spiritual Teacher will not pass or fail you. Quite the contrary, a spiritual Teacher's commitment is to escort you to your goal, no matter how long it takes or how much effort it requires. The spiritual Teacher will stay with his student until the student achieves his goal.

The Teacher and the Path

Just what is the experience of a spiritual Teacher like?

First of all, it is my observation that in life we are always thrown into one of two roles—teacher or student. Rarely are we placed in a position of being a neutral, non-participating observer who is unaffected by surrounding words and actions. Even in something as "everyday" as getting together with the guys for a cup of morning coffee—we may be talking about sports, politics, God or whatever—there is a sharing of information going on, at which time we are either influenced by the opinions of others, i.e., we are students, or we influence others with our opinions, i.e., we are teachers.

Also, in the course of life we are learning the art of communicating in consciousness. A silent communication always accompanies our outer conversations with individuals that either validates or invalidates the outer conversation. For example, you may go to a car dealer and hear just the words you hope to hear, "This is absolutely the lowest price I can offer and the lowest price you'll find anywhere." Inwardly, however, you don't trust the words. The inner communication does not affirm the outer communication, so you end up doubting the entire experience.

On the other side of this spectrum, we've probably all had the experience of meeting someone very briefly, perhaps for just a few minutes, but we immediately care for and trust that individual. We are simply drawn to that person. Here the inner communication affirms the outer experience, even when very little outer communication has taken place.

This ability to communicate in consciousness is what truly empowers our life experiences. Have you ever had the

> Concentrate to lengthen your consciousness-realm. Meditate to heighten your consciousness-sky. Contemplate to deepen your consciousness-sea.
>
> s.c.

opportunity to speak with someone for whom you genuinely care, when they are a little bit down in the dumps? Think about how you feel and react. Let's say your dearest and closest friend is a little depressed and you run into them at the local café. Immediately upon greeting them, you know that there is something wrong. It's not the words, but you can read it in the person's face and feel it inside yourself. What do you do then?

If you are like most, you'll affirm your love for that person by talking to them and you'll make a sincere effort to lift them out of their depression and into a happier space. You hope that by injecting them with your love and concern you can lift their consciousness. To the extent that we all do this, we are all little "gurus in training", because this is exactly what the spiritual Teacher does, that is, he tries to lift the consciousness of the seeker-student!

Now imagine that instead of a limited amount of love and concern, you had at your disposal an ocean's worth. Furthermore, imagine that the joy level you could access was not merely that of earthly contentment, but heavenly bliss. These are the tools of the spiritual Teacher who is motivated by exactly the same force that you display for your friend—love.

> "My God, how old are You?"
> "My child, I shall tell you. But first, tell Me how old you are?"
> "I am just a year old."
> "My child, if you are a year old, I am one day younger than you and one day older than you; one day younger than you in imperfection and one day older than you in perfection. Give Me half the imperfection that you have and take from Me half the perfection that I have. Let us be fully equal."
> "What will happen, my God, if You and I become fully equal?"
> "My child, when we two become fully equal, you will be known as another God and I will be known as another man."
>
> S.C.

When encountering a spiritual Teacher, it may be natural to anticipate the encounter with both a little excitement and perhaps even a little discomfort because you are treading into new and previously uncharted territory. We tend to judge others in terms of our own experience. We don't know infinite love, so how is it possible for someone else to know? In fact, the encounter is typically quite the opposite. When you find your spiritual Teacher, it is usually associated with a sense of arriving home and a sense of security.

Here it is important to consider your own spiritual process. Today, as a result of your aspiration, you have begun the process of expanding your consciousness. Tomorrow, you shall grow and ultimately realise the highest Truth. The day after tomorrow, someone else might achieve the same goal. That means that yesterday, someone else could have achieved this same realisation before you. This is exactly what the spiritual Teacher represents—someone who has achieved the goal just a day before you. As such, he is an elder brother of humanity.

> In the outer world willingness to learn is a good start. In the inner world willingness to learn is a splendid victory.
>
> — S.C.

It is important to note that the process of which I spoke in the last chapter, the process of progressing from instinct to curiosity—ultimately through conscious aspiration—this process need *not* be linear. One need not be relatively advanced in spiritual progress in order to encounter and experience a spiritual Teacher. You see, unlike an outer school where your acceptance is based on previous accomplishment, a spiritual Teacher looks only to see if the seeker is willing to climb the spiritual ladder. It is not one's accomplishment but rather one's willingness that is much, much more important.

There was a time when as a younger man I wrote a column called "In the Spirit" for a New Age magazine. I was a kind of spiritual Ann Landers. I would regularly receive letters from seekers who would typically write something such as, "I really want to embark upon a spiritual life, but ..." and here the list gets pretty long,

... I am not ready.

... I am not pure enough.

... I have no discipline.

... I can't quiet my mind.

... but, but, but, etc., etc., etc.

My response was always the same. "You are putting the cart before the horse." You adopt a spiritual life not because you have these qualities, but because you need these qualities. If aspiration and sincerity are present, you have the necessary prerequisites.

So, what is the experience like and just how does it work? Please allow me to place before you the most often asked questions that I have received in my classes about the experience.

Is a Teacher necessary?

Interestingly, whenever Sri Chinmoy is asked this question, he always answers, "No," and then qualifies it by saying that the first person to realise God, obviously, did not have a spiritual Teacher. He would also comment that if a seeker is extremely advanced, God himself may play the role of Teacher for that seeker. But in practical terms, this caliber of seeker is extremely rare, and they probably arrived at this point by having had a spiritual Teacher at an earlier point in their spiritual-aspiration career. From my perspective, I look at history's greatest souls. According to *The Aquarian Gospel*, the Christ had teachers all along his re-awakening. Sri Ramakrishna had teachers in his youth, and my own Teacher, Sri Chinmoy, was guided into the higher states of consciousness by Sri Aurobindo. It did not require much humility on my part to accept that if these great souls had spiritual Teachers, perhaps I might need one as well.

> " Your willingness to transform your own life is fast transforming the world around you. Something more: Your willingness is the fruit of God's fondest Concern for your life's climbing journey.
>
> — S.C.

I find it curious that for some of the most mundane tasks, we recognize the need for a teacher. Do you want to correct that hook in your golf swing? Or learn French? Or learn how to weave? For all these things, a teacher is a given. But for spiritual progress, to climb the highest mountain of God-realisation, for this we don't need a teacher? Admittedly, one could learn French, correct a golf swing or master a computer program by oneself, but the speed at which you could do these things would be a lot slower and a lot more painstaking.

A few years ago, while running along the paths by Lake Michigan, I saw so many roller bladers of different ages, sizes and shapes that I was inspired to give it a try. As a child, I roller skated quite regularly and anticipated it wouldn't be too difficult. So, off I went to purchase a pair of reasonably-priced, entry-level skates. I have to tell you, I experienced so much child-like joy skating around, especially on level, nicely paved surfaces. I would go out every day and, after a few weeks, got to a point where I was reasonably comfortable on my skates. Still, going downhill was a bit frightening. I would describe myself to be on the klutzy-cautious side.

On one particular day, I saw an ad for roller-blading lessons. It offered the option of group lessons. Unfortunately, the times for the less expensive group lessons didn't fit, so I splurged for a private lesson. I was anticipating my lesson with excitement. Up pulls a van, and a tall, young fellow steps out. I watched him as he donned his skates and immediately started skating backwards while putting on the other regalia: helmet, elbow pads, knee pads, wrist support. He wasn't showing off; it was simply a matter of him being completely comfortable and experienced. Seeing him skate, I was immediately confident in his skills and inspired about the upcoming lesson.

Onto my lesson. He taught me how to think on my skates. New words and methods became part of my experience—edging, pressure and shifting my centre of gravity. Then the best part; he taught me how to stop properly! In a single two hour session, I learned a year's worth of skating. True, I probably could have learned everything he taught me by trial and error, but it would have taken much, much longer with the expense of a lot more falls and bruises.

Such is the value of a true teacher. When you experience a true spiritual Teacher, he embodies the very things that you aspire to achieve in your own life. This takes the goal out of the realm of spiritual fantasy and makes it much more tangible and accessible.

A true spiritual Teacher must have achieved a certain level of illumination, and in this aspect, absolute purity must be present; a spiritual Teacher's life must be an embodiment of his teachings. I see with my own two eyes the kind of human being I want to become in my own spiritual Teacher, Sri Chinmoy.

A spiritual path

The sum total of the spiritual Teacher's teachings is what is referred to as a "path", and this is a perfect word. If you've ever done any trekking or hiking, you know the value of a clear-cut path. It creates a confidence on the part of the hiker that he is indeed going in the correct direction. Furthermore, just the existence of a path can provide impetus to walk it.

> "Why do we accept a spiritual path? We accept a spiritual path just because we feel that if we walk along the path, eventually we shall reach a destination which is flooded with all the divine qualities of the absolute Supreme.
>
> S.C.

During my first visit in Myanmar (the former Burma), our hotel was located right next to a large lake. The good runners would regularly report about this incredible 10-mile path around the lake. I was inspired by their experience and felt safe that if there was indeed a path, I could certainly make 10 miles, even if I had to walk. The very fact that there was a path inspired me to try it.

What was of particular interest was that I was running very successfully until the path disappeared! I was at a corner and the lake was no longer in sight, so I was no longer sure what direction to take. Hesitation entered into me. I thought, "If I take the wrong direction, I might be out for hours!" I committed myself to a hard right turn and within 100 meters I started to walk, all because I lost the path! About two miles down that road, I recognized where I was and that, indeed, I was on the correct road, so I started to run again. A week later, confident with knowledge of the path, I tried it again and ran the entire way.

Having a path is so helpful. You know when you are on it and equally important, you know when you are not! Remember when you attended school, in any grade. I'll use college as an example.

You declare a major, i.e., you decide on a goal; "I want to be a bio-medical engineer." Then a path is laid out. You have to take course A, B and C in this order. You need teachers along the way to guide you along the path. With appropriate discipline and study, you accomplish your goal.

The teacher and the path are even more important in achieving spiritual goals because, unlike being an engineer where there are many examples, the achievement of self-mastery or God-realisation is very rare. We don't know what the goal looks like or, perhaps even more troublesome, we don't know how to get there.

How does a spiritual Teacher actually teach?

The process of learning occurs in a number of different ways, although a single vehicle is present in all of these. (What is that vehicle? Please indulge me. I'll save it for the end of this chapter!)

Whenever you spend time with an individual or group of friends, you are affected by the consciousness of these people. When you spend time with someone who is happy and upbeat, you come away "happified" by the experience. Conversely, should you spend time with someone who is down and depressed, it is not unusual for you to be a bit tainted by that depression. Herein lies the merit of group meditation and associating with others who are aspiring. The collective consciousness impacts the individual consciousness.

This is most certainly true when interacting with a spiritual Teacher. When I simply spend time with my own teacher, I come away spiritualized by the interaction. He may not be interacting outwardly with me at all! Simply being in the presence of that consciousness lifts my own. I come away seeing myself in a more spiritual light. This phenomenon is perhaps the most important thing that a spiritual Teacher does: to convince the seeker of the reality of his own spirituality. This is so important because the more one believes in his own spirituality, the more one acts in accordance with it. And the more one acts in accordance with it, the more it makes itself felt in the seeker, thus setting up a wonderful upward spiral in the direction of spiritual progress.

Secondly, as I mentioned earlier, the spiritual Teacher will present the seeker with a path. The path is a set of wisdom-guidelines for the seeker to follow. For example, on Sri Chinmoy's path I am a vegetarian, I run, I read, I study my Teacher's writings, I meditate every day a number of times, I attend group meditation and more. These are all part of the path, to which each of his student-seekers apply themselves.

Again, each of us is an individual, and the wonderful thing about having a spiritual Teacher is that he can guide you individually. There is a wonderful story attributed to Sri Ramakrishna. He had two disciples who both had a similar experience—they both overheard some people speaking ill of Sri Ramakrishna. Now, one of these disciples had a very mild disposition—quiet, perhaps a bit shy. The second disciple had just the opposite temperament—he tended to be a bit angry and volatile.

Interestingly, to the one who was mild, Sri Ramakrishna counseled, "Where is your conviction? Why did you not defend me?" To the one who was angry, he said, "Where is your patience and forgiveness? You should not let these things upset you." Each encountered the same experience, but two different teachings were applied. This makes perfect sense. We all have unique dispositions and the spiritual Teacher will customise his teachings to suit our particular inner needs, weaknesses and strengths.

These inner issues and their resolutions need not be mediated by actual conversation. The domain of consciousness is not bound by space and time. How many times have we heard or experienced stories such as that of the mother who just "knew" something had happened to her child?

When I was in chiropractic school, for some reason, I was drawn into the politics of administration-student issues and my fellow students convinced me to run for student council president. In general, this is very much unlike me. I have no particular fondness for politics. At any rate, I won the election and assumed the role. Immediately, I regretted it. Here was a task that could easily (and probably more effectively!) be performed by someone else. It was taking up much of my time—time that I would normally have spent on my spiritual life. I was meditating just a bit less, offering fewer meditation classes, that sort of thing. I regretted having taken on the task but figured that for a year, I would deal with it. Day-by-day it got worse.

About a month or so later, I received a message from Sri Chinmoy, "Good boy, you're putting too much time in your chiropractic life and not enough time in your spiritual life." This message came out of the blue, or so it seemed. No one had spoken to Guru about my situation. Somehow, some way, he simply knew. The next day I turned my post over to the vice president. My legacy was the creation of the student newspaper, appropriately called *The Spinal Column*. Ugh!

There is one final means of teaching. I mentioned earlier that there was a common vehicle present in the teacher's methodology. Well, this subject will still have to wait a little longer.

Why not learn from many teachers?

I am often asked, "Why *one* Teacher?" In other words, doesn't it make sense to have many teachers and learn from all of them? Well, at first consideration, while this may *seem* to make sense, the answer to this question is quite simply, "No." There is a saying that you are more likely to strike oil by digging one well deep rather than 50 wells shallow. It is true that there are many paths up the mountain and any one of them will take you there. One path may be very steep, while another may wind back and forth. Yet another may be lined with flowers. The seeker's task is to find the path that is best suited to them, and then climb that path. Seeking out the guidance of many different teachers is the same as walking around the base of the mountain and taking a few steps up each path. While this process may be necessary to initially find your proper path, in fact, once you do find it, it is best to concentrate on your particular path to reach the summit. You may turn your head on occasion and respectfully acknowledge those walking on other paths, but your concentration and focus should be on your own road.

Sri Chinmoy is fond of using the boat/boatman metaphor and this works well. He says that each teacher is like a boatman whose task it is to take those who are in his boat to the goal. Let us expand this image. Imagine that the task is to reach the Atlantic Ocean. You could be in a boat on the Mississippi River, and the boatman instructs you to row south and only south. For those in his boat, clearly this is the correct direction. On the other hand, if you were in a boat on the Delaware River, the boatman would instruct you to row east and only east, as this will take you to the goal. Both teachers are absolutely correct for the people who are in their particular boats. But, by honouring both teachings, one can easily become confused. Or, one may think, "Well, this teacher says to go south, while this one says to go east. I bet its faster to go southeast!" That simply is not true. That person will end up walking a long way and probably become discouraged long before he arrives at the goal!

So, the seeker's task is to find the path that best suits him and then to walk that path. In actuality, the process of finding a teacher is actually a little bit of a misrepresentation. The seeker and teacher actually find each other.

How do I find a Teacher?

Sri Chinmoy responds to this question by saying that if you are attracted to a number of different teachers, one should very soulfully chant the name of the teacher in their hearts and feel which one gives them the most joy. Allow me to confess that this would not have worked for me, because I was a "spiritual zero" when I encountered Guru and wouldn't recognize spiritual joy if it slapped me in the face! In practical terms, you must apply yourself to the path. You may look at a restaurant and it may appear very beautiful to you, but the real test is to taste the food.

This process is much like applying to a college or university. You apply to a particular college because its program suits you. For example, suppose that you are interested in studying music.

> "To achieve realisation oneself and alone is like crossing the ocean in a raft. But to achieve realisation through the Grace of a Guru is like crossing the ocean in a swift and strong boat, which ferries you safely across the sea of ignorance to the Golden Shore. — s.c.

There may be three or four different universities that have programs that interest you. You visit the campus and talk with other students and faculty. You may eliminate one school and then decide on a best choice and apply. The school then assesses you—your qualifications, your grades—and perhaps even interviews you.

Just as there must be mutual acceptance between a university and a prospective student, so must there be mutual acceptance between a spiritual Teacher and a seeker. You may attend a program in which the meditation emphasises the mind, while another emphasises the heart. Let us say, the heart path appeals to you. Then, your Teacher must also accept you. If he is a genuine Teacher, he will acknowledge that his path is not for every seeker and it is a great injustice if he accepts a seeker who is not intended for his path. (Frankly, the Teacher is in a much better position than the student to assess whether the student is suitable for his path. I've experienced many seekers who apply to Sri Chinmoy to be students simply based on the faith that, if he accepts them as a student, then it is the right place.)

Again, I want to emphasise that the spiritual Teacher's assessment of the student is not based necessarily on inner accomplishment. It is based on communion with the soul of the individual as to the student's readiness and willingness.

When a seeker is accepted by a Teacher, the student must then apply himself to the path. Not to do so would be the equivalent of being accepted to a college and then not attending class. The student should expect that there will be many things on the path that he might not yet understand. If your Teacher is genuinely illumined, he will see many things in the seeker that the seeker does not see in himself! It is like the toddler taking his first steps. The parent knows that the child should initiate the task of walking. The child has no idea, only enthusiasm for the task. But the parent puts the child on two feet and encourages him to walk, sometimes months before the muscles are ready!

It is only natural that based on the seeker's own life experience, he will readily understand some things asked of him. Some things get a "maybe," while other things are totally new. The seeker's task is *not* to accept and reject. The seeker's task is to taste and test to see if the teachings bear fruit in his life.

If they do, then two things happen. First, bearing fruit means that the seeker's consciousness is elevated and with that, he sees things very differently. Secondly, by virtue of this experience, the bridge of faith is being built and, based on that faith, a new willingness develops.

But I want to do this by myself...

While it is true that you could accomplish this all by yourself without the help of a Teacher, the fact is that it is much, much more difficult. I think that sometimes people have a fear of letting someone else into their inner space. Ironically, the fact is that we are letting people in all the time! Frankly, until one has spent time in meditation and inner discipline, our inner space is very vulnerable and porous. You can be walking down the street and pass someone who is extremely depressed, and without being aware of the cause, your own thoughts become depressed! Consider how a simple sound bite from an ad agency can create a desire in you for the product. In my teenage years when I smoked, every time I saw an ad for a cigarette, regardless of the brand, I felt compelled to light one up. I realised that the ad was not intended to make me change brand, it was simply intended to make me light up.

> " The Guru is at once the source of his disciple's achievements and a most faithful servant of his disciple's love. ᔐ s.c.

So the consideration should be not whether or not to let someone else into your inner space, but rather (1) to filter those

225

who you let in, and (2) consciously choose to let someone in who is in a position to illumine your consciousness.

In truth, the Teacher does not let you relinquish your responsibilities. Instead he guides you, encourages you and perhaps coaches you in how to achieve the goal.

When climbing a new and challenging mountain, an experienced mountaineer will take a guide who knows the path. At a crossroads, that guide may say, "This is the right direction," or "This is the safest path for you." But the guide does not climb for you. In exactly the same way, a spiritual Teacher will guide you in the direction you should take to climb the inner mountain. Knowing that there is a steep grade up ahead, he may tell you to exercise your quadriceps at a lower level. In other words, he may help you to develop some patience or forgiveness in preparation for a more difficult trial which looms further along your spiritual path.

> Lord, I do not know. Do teach me! "Son, first unlearn what you have so far learned. I shall then not only teach you but also make you another god like Me."
>
> — S.C.

You might think of a spiritual Teacher as a coach, or perhaps in this era, I might say a "personal trainer". When you have a coach, you surrender decisions to him. For example, let's say you are training to run a fast mile. Today you might be scheduled for ten 100-meter sprints, but you wake up in the morning and just don't feel like it. But, alas, your coach is out there saying, "Let's go," so you are there for the exercise. I meditate by 6 a.m. everyday (or earlier). I must confess to you that if it were not for Sri Chinmoy coaching me to take up this task, I doubt that I would do it with the same regularity.

I particularly enjoyed an experience that a fellow student of Sri Chinmoy shared with me. Many of my friends have swum the

English Channel. This one young woman told me that when it finally came to doing the swim, the experience itself reminded her of her relationship with Guru. She told me that she practised five hours a day in preparation for the channel swim. On the actual day of the swim, obviously it was she who put one arm in front of the other and swam the entire 21-mile length of the English Channel. She did all the work. Then she added this point—you cannot swim the English Channel without having a boat next to you, guiding you along the way. You simply can't do it. For one thing, it's illegal. But again, can you imagine the likelihood of getting across without the boat? Twenty-one miles of the coldest, murkiest water, swimming sometimes at night?! She told me that during the entire swim, all she did was follow the light on the boat, which set the course. In no way did having the boat there diminish the necessity of her effort or training. But the presence of the boat guided her and certainly made her feel more secure in her remarkable task.

In exactly the same way, having a spiritual Teacher in no way negates your personal effort or responsibility. It is you who must perform the disciplines and it is you who will reap the rewards. Your task is simply to allow yourself to be guided.

Finally, allow me to share a humorous but serious saying (and please forgive me, it is not my intention to offend anyone). "He who takes himself as a teacher, has a fool as a student!"

Is it you who is taking the teacher?

Thus far, we've explored the "acceptance of the teacher" from our own personal perspective, but there is another vantage point, a very important one at that. In preparation for this discussion, I would like you to perform a very important meditation.

Exercise / **Meditation on God**

Recall that the very premise upon which all of this is founded is that God, the Supreme, the Universal Consciousness, exists inside you. Nay, not only exists, but is your own highest nature. Throughout this book, I've offered a number of meditation exercises to access this. For this exercise, let's just cut to the chase. God exists inside you. God is your own highest part. Well, find it, experience it. Yes, you read correctly, find and experience the God inside yourself. I do not care what technique you choose to use. If you feel chanting will accomplish the task, then chant. Eyes open? Eyes closed? Your choice. Sit up, lie down—it's up to you. Whatever method or technique you want, do whatever it takes to discover the God inside you, to know it. Please approach this exercise seriously, as it is an important exercise. How does God present him/her/itself to you? Take three to five minutes to do this. You can spend more time if you are inspired to do so.

I do this exercise in every class. It is my favorite exercise because it brings me right back to the essential task at hand. Sometimes my own meditations degenerate into inner chats (or even gripe sessions!), but this exercise always brings me home. I find that whenever I do this exercise, at some point my mind blows a fuse. I begin to think about it, but thought cannot take me where I want to go. My mind surrenders. At this point, I am left to my heart. I've done this exercise in hundreds of classes. It's valuable to share the responses that people have given. Here it's important to note not only the response, but also the tone with which the response is given, which I will dialog about shortly.

God is:

- Light
- Energy
- Peace
- The Creator
- My highest part
- That thing that creates connectivity
- My source
- The spirit in all things
- Love
- My father
- The common substance of everything
- A universal consciousness
- Warmth
- Protection

This is just a brief list. I am sure you can enlarge this list with your own experience. Indeed, each person's answer is 100 percent legitimate for that particular person, at that particular time. And, responses might change at a different time. But what is present in the tone, and admittedly, what is almost impossible to convey in the written word, is that people respond to this with an uncertainty, or even a question. They simply won't say, "God is my higher self." They'll say, "Well, um, er, uh—God is my higher self?" or "I think, God is light?"

My favorite answer of all time happened in a class of about 30 people. Starting one at a time from the rear of the class I asked each for a response. The final person, a woman in the front row, confessed, "You know, I actually forgot the question." And that is the problem—we all forget the question at some point.

The classic story about describing God is that of the blind men groping at the elephant. One grabs the ear and declares,

"Aha, the elephant is like a thick carpet." Another grabs the tail saying, "No, it is like a rope." Still another grabs the leg and corrects the first two, "No, it is like a tree trunk." And, the last one misses the elephant altogether affirming, "The elephant does not exist." They are all right according to their own experience, but of course, the elephant is far greater than any of their individual experiences. (In another version of this story, the blind men fight over whose vision of God is correct!)

> I am not totally lost, although my mind is blind and my heart is blindfolded. ✍ S.C.

Similarly, God is what we experience and again far greater than anything we might conceive, even when combined with the perceptions of others.

Poor God. Why do I say that? Let us assume that the two essential spiritual principles which form the basis for this book are true:

1) God exists.
2) The purpose of our human life is to achieve union with God.

Clearly, assuming both of these statements are true, then they are also related. If God exists, then God also created the purpose! God created the necessity for humanity to have union with Him. I repeat again, poor God. He sees a seeker who is ripe for that union, who wants to approach God (in whatever form), but God also sees that the seeker hardly knows how to think of God, no less achieve union with Him. So what does God do? He says, "Let me place before the seeker someone who can expedite his journey."

There is an ancient saying, "When the student is ready, the Teacher appears." We might think in terms of taking on a Teacher, but I think something else is happening. I view the spiritual Teacher as a grace placed before me by God, as an expression of God's own necessity to enable a more conscious union with humanity.

You see, we are already versed in the ability to communicate in consciousness. It is actually much easier for us to communicate in consciousness with a human who is fully identified with the Divine, then it is for us to approach the Divine itself. Ergo, the necessity of a Teacher.

Communion in consciousness

This is the primary and most important vehicle of teaching about which I spoke earlier. It permeates the other methods and is the primary tool by which the Teacher illumines the seeker-student.

Let me share my personal perspective on a most significant experience in the life of the Christ to demonstrate what I mean. I refer to the Christ because in the West we are more familiar with his life than other great Masters. Although he is not my spiritual Teacher, I have a deep love and adoration for the Christ.

> A real Guru is the selfless, dedicated and eternal beggar who begs omnipotence and omnipresence from God to feed his unconsciously hungry and consciously aspiring disciples, in perfect conformity with their soul's needs. — S.C.

One of the most poignant moments in his life, nay, in perhaps all of spiritual history, occurs in the crucifixion of the Christ. Let's relive this. Here was a man, teacher, Avatar whose intention was to demonstrate a purer love and compassion to humanity, and what was his fate? Consider what it felt like to be hung on a cross with spikes in hands and feet. Can we not understand his utterance, "My Lord, why hast thou forsaken me?" How many times do we say this same thing when, despite our best efforts, things just don't go that well? This is the cry of humanity.

But then, consider the next utterance of the Christ, "My Lord, forgive them for they know not what they do." How much love must Christ have had for humanity to have uttered these immortal words? This is the full power of love—unconditional love. And this is the descending Grace.

We see that both the cry of humanity and the Grace of Divinity live side-by-side in the genuine spiritual Teacher. The Teacher is someone who is at once human, but at the same time, someone whose consciousness is already merged with the infinite. He is a link, or a bridge over which humanity can cross. On one side of the bridge is humanity's cry for the highest, and on the other side of the bridge is God's Grace. We, as seekers, cross over that bridge; we "pass through" the Teacher by virtue of our communion in consciousness. This passing through the teacher is prominent throughout spiritual history:

From The Christ to his apostles :
> *"I am the way, the truth, and the life: no man cometh unto the Father, but by me."*

From Sri Krishna to his disciple Arjuna:
> *"I am the goal of the wise man, I am the way."*
> *"I am the end of the path, the witness, the Lord, the sustainer."*
> *"Fill your heart and mind with me, adore me, make all your acts an offering to me, bow down to me in self-surrender. If you set your heart upon me thus, and take me for your ideal above all others, you will come into my Being."*

From Lord Buddha to his devotees:

> *"You are my children, I am your father; through me you*
> *have been released from your sufferings. I myself having*
> *reached the other shore, help others to cross the stream;*
> *I myself having attained salvation, am a saviour to*
> *others; being comforted, I comfort others and lead them*
> *to the place of refuge."*

Sri Chinmoy, my Teacher, is my bridge. In my own Teacher's words from his book *My Flute*, I offer two poems which beautifully demonstrate both sides of the bridge—on one side, the cry of a lost seeker, and on the other side, the eternal aspect of one fully identified with the God-nature:

A Little

A little joy have I of ceaseless joy,
> *A little day of timeless day.*
Yet knows no bound this empty show of mine;
> *I march along a goalless way.*

O Love! A desert within me ever pines.
> *Do turn it into a song of dawn.*
I know not in what hour of evil night
> *Thou art, my Lord, from me withdrawn.*

Life now must reach Thy Breath of Bliss supreme,
> *Make Thee the one and only Guide.*
Thou art the Bridge between my death and birth;
> *O let my longings in Thee abide.*

The Absolute

"No mind, no form, I only exist;
　　Now ceased all will and thought;
The final end of Nature's dance,
　　I am it whom I have sought.

A realm of Bliss bare, ultimate;
　　Beyond both knower and known;
A rest immense I enjoy at last;
　　I face the One alone.

I have crossed the secret ways of life,
　　I have become the Goal.
The Truth immutable is revealed;
　　I am the way, the God-Soul.

My spirit aware of all the heights,
　　I am mute in the core of the Sun.
I barter nothing with time and deeds;
　　My cosmic play is done.

And so, it is by crossing over, or passing through the Teacher, that we attain to God. The communion in consciousness between teacher and student is the primary vehicle by which they both fulfil themselves. When I read my Teacher's writings, I receive the wisdom and inspiration of his words. But even more important, I am creating a portal of entry into his consciousness, through which I can pass into the God-nature.

I close with this thought. Time is the most precious gift. We can divide time into infinitely many moments. It makes sense that we should live each moment to its utmost, which for me means to aspire to the heights at every moment.

Yes, time is precious, time is sacred. Wherever you are, start your spiritual journey. Find your spiritual path.

Allow me to close with a passage from Sri Chinmoy's writings, from his book, *The Wings of Joy*:

Start Here and Now

“In order to become one with God, you have to consciously start your spiritual journey. Here and Now is the soul's motto. If you have not yet started, then your soul wants you to start your spiritual journey at this very moment. If you have doubt with regard to God's existence, no harm. Doubt as much as you want to. Eventually, you will become tired of doubting God. If you doubt the existence of inner peace and bliss, doubt as long as you want to. Even if you have doubts with regard to the inner life or God's reality, it is best to start your inner journey anyway.

If you are curious to know what spirituality is, you can accept spirituality with your utmost curiosity. See if it is just superficially fascinating or if it is something deep and vast, to which you can devote your entire life. You may start with curiosity, but soon your curiosity will turn into real aspiration. If you enter the spiritual life because others have done so, this is also fine. If you see that somebody's life has become peaceful and happy after he has accepted the spiritual life, there is nothing wrong with imitating him...

...If you still cherish doubt or curiosity, then start with doubt, start with curiosity. But start! Step by step, you will be able to march toward your goal. God is already eager to have you. You may not be eager to have God, but God the eternal Father, God the eternal Mother, is crying for you. You must make the *decision that you want God. If you really want God, then start where you are—here and now. The goal of conscious oneness with God the infinite Light and infinite Truth shall be yours.*

> *Your heart's cry is a real treasure.*
> *Your heart's cry flies like an eagle*
> *To reach the highest goal of your purest soul.*

(The Wings of Joy, "Start Here and Now")

I have written another book called, *At the Feet of my Master*. This book is a collection of stories and experiences which resulted from the unique role I had which offered me the opportunity to sit at the Master's feet—literally! What follows in this chapter is a selection of just a few of those stories.

As I mentioned in the introduction of this book, many people have told me that these stories convey more effectively the role and nature of the student—teacher relationship than all of the philosophising of the earlier pages.

At the Feet of my Master

I, along with three or four other "doctorish" boys, worked on Guru's legs in an attempt to resolve his never-ending leg pain. Guru's legs seemed to bear the brunt of his duties as spiritual Teacher, and they were in constant pain.

Please understand that the position of sitting at the

Master's feet is a time-honoured, sacred position and opportunity and, as a result, the boys who performed this task were often perceived by others as being special in some way.

Forgive me, but my perspective is different. Blessed, yes—special, no. I simply had the remarkably good fortune to be given this role by Sri Chinmoy. He could easily have chosen someone else.

I do know one thing. I can never be grateful enough for this special opportunity that was presented to me. I simply do not know how.

⊙ NOAMS: No Outer Attention Misery Syndrome

This is a story which has many lessons and experiences associated with it. One thing I've learned over the years is that God does not have time to waste time with my life. Every moment has its purpose. I, on the other hand, have an uncanny capacity to waste my time, or so it seems. But God uses even my worst moments to His best advantage! The story that follows and the lessons that came with it were years in the making.

When I first became a student, I felt there was no necessity to speak with Guru, and therefore never sought to do so. For five years, I never initiated a word with Guru, even though I was the leader of one of his Centres. Sometimes he would pass by and say, "You are all right?" or something like that, but it was rarely more than that.

One year, during a Christmas trip in Bermuda, I was talking with a friend of mine who was also the leader of another Midwest Centre. He told me that every time he visited New York to see Guru, he requested an interview and got it. This, frankly, awoke the jealousy-flame in me, so I decided I would ask for an interview, and to my surprise and joy I received it!

This was the very dawn of an outer relationship with Guru that twisted, turned, and became richer and more purposeful over the years. Many brother and sister students admired those who would appear to have a closer outer role with Guru than they might have had. But in fact, that role would only be there if it were necessary for the progress of the student. It is not any indication of the Master's affection for the student. He is not bound by such things.

As a student of more than forty years, I have witnessed that Guru gave you just what you needed at just the right time. If it served your aspiration-progress to have an outer relationship with you, Guru would carve one out, and he did so at the appropriate time. However, some students are better suited to a purely inner relationship, and that is precisely what Guru cultivated.

Parallel to this, it has also been my observation that rarely does the student ever get what he thinks that he needs, deserves or wants. When someone else gets attention and you don't, you feel miserable. Even if you get outer attention, you want more. And sometimes you get outer attention when you don't want it. All of these experiences are symptoms of a common syndrome. I call this syndrome, "No Outer Attention Misery Syndrome," or NOAMS, for short.

But back to my story. In the early 1970's, as a result of a bad fall, Guru injured his back and developed a severe sciatica down his left

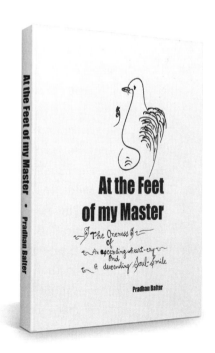

At the Feet of my Master • Pradhan Balter

At the Feet of my Master

The Oneness of
An ascending heart-cry
And
A descending Soul-Smile

Pradhan Balter

leg. He also subsequently developed a "foot slap" on his right side which became apparent whenever he ran, a fitness activity he loved to do. When he placed his right foot down, it would quickly drop, making a slapping noise as it did so. Guru was regularly receiving various kinds of treatment and leg massage to try to relieve it.

I was a chiropractor, and in casual conversation I mentioned to my friend, Savyasachi, that I thought chiropractic treatments might fix Guru's problem. I want to emphasise that I was not at all seeking to do it. Neither did I feel qualified nor spiritually pure enough to work on Guru. Well, apparently Savyasachi mentioned my suggestion to Guru, because the next morning, in front of a number of students, and in a very public place, I was shocked when Guru called me forward to treat him chiropractically, and then work and massage his painful legs. Honestly, sitting at Guru's feet for the first time, I was surprised and nervous.

This moment was the beginning of a different and more obvious outer relationship with Guru. Soon I became Guru's main visiting masseur, and with this new role came an entire new set of experiences. You see, before this time I was pretty much an unknown, an obscure ex-New York student now living in Chicago. Now I was suddenly thrust front and centre, working on my spiritual Teacher. Not only did my relationship with Guru suddenly change, but my relationship with everyone else did too. There is a reason for this. As I mentioned earlier, from an historical perspective, occupying the seat at your Teacher's feet is a time-honoured and most sacred position. Suddenly, the person known as Pradhan garnered a new respect from his student-family.

Everybody looked at me differently. In fact, even my fellow Chicago students were affected by it. Once, a Canadian approached a young girl in our Centre, "What's it like to work with him?"

"With who?" she responded.

"You know, with him, Pradhan?"

The girl was dumbfounded (rightfully so) and said, "I dunno... he tells a lot of jokes?" She was searching for an answer and couldn't quite figure out why she was being asked.

Much more importantly (and inappropriately), the dreaded disease started. I came to use this role as a gauge for Guru's affection for me. As long as I was at Guru's feet, I was okay. If not, something was wrong—clearly Guru was upset with me. As a result of all this, a not so subtle pride-attachment developed. Yes, I became very attached to the role.

Every year at Christmas time, Sri Chinmoy traveled to some part of the world with a group of students. Well, one Christmas took us to Japan. There Guru had me accompany him everywhere he went. I was carrying his bags, reserving seats and working on his legs at every opportunity. I was in outer-attention-bliss syndrome. (This is a close relation to NOAMS, but is much more delusional.)

The following year, our Christmas trip brought us to Venezuela, and I was looking forward to playing the same role. I was in for a surprise. Guru did not speak to me. Not one word. And with that, day by day, I was becoming more miserable. Of course, no one knew this. I dared not share it with anybody out of embarrassment. Nevertheless, it was there with me, growing deeper and deeper every day.

There were three or four boys who played this role on the trip. I remember one fateful evening Guru called out for one of those boys, Nirvik. Now, I knew that none of these boys were around, so I quickly yelled out, "He's not here, Guru!"

"Not here? All right, is Savyasachi here then?"

"He's not here either, Guru," came my voice.

One by one, Guru called for other boys to work on his leg, and over and over my voice was heard, "He's not here."

Finally, there was just me left. I waited. And waited. After a thoughtful pause Guru said, "All right, since there is no one here to massage my leg, let's go downstairs to the other room."

Ugh. I was in agony, devastated. Clearly I had fallen and I was in the abyss. Everyone went downstairs except for me. I remained upstairs with my head in my hands. A few moments later I heard someone's voice. It was one of the girls who regularly cook for Guru. She told me, "Guru said you should bring down his chair."

"He did!?" and I did just that. Little did I know that this was an omen of what was to come.

Days passed and still I was not called by Guru. My misery quietly and privately grew with each day.

It was now New Year's Eve, and Guru held a beautiful meditation under a clear moon on the veranda outside the hotel. Afterwards, he gave a significant talk while Nirvik worked on his leg, and then Guru asked for questions. Ashrita was the first to raise his hand and ask a question which Guru answered. Then the moment came—I asked a question. Well, Guru did not answer my question. Instead, with a very serious tone, I was greeted with, "Good boy, what you need is an entirely new attitude towards your spiritual life."

From the seriousness of Guru's tone, I knew this was the big one. I immediately began shrinking inwardly and tried to shrink outwardly. He continued, "Here you are suffering so much. You're so miserable because Nirvik is massaging my leg and I haven't asked you to massage me. You think that I don't care for you, that I don't love you. Everything is demand, demand, demand."

He went on. "You have to feel at every moment that I know what is best for you and at every moment that I love you. If today I smile at you, you have to feel 'Today Guru is showing his love for me by smiling at me,' and tomorrow if I don't smile at you, you should feel 'My Guru is showing his love for me by not smiling at me.' "

This is the condensed version of Guru's response but it captures the essence. Now you have to remember that this message was being powerfully reinforced by the fact that inwardly Guru had been perfectly reading my inner misery. Without my telling him, he clearly saw my attachment-suffering, so I was easily convinced that even without the outer communication, he knew what was happening in my life.

Guru wasn't finished. It went on to be a general talk to everybody about selflessness and about demanding. This was the start of a number of messages given to all of us, spanning a period of years, about selfless giving without any expectation of return.

Anyway, it was a serious scolding. It was the kind of scolding that brought my friends over to me saying things like, "You know, if you weren't so strong, Guru wouldn't have done that publicly," as they patted me on the back. Someone actually sent flowers to my room anonymously!

When Guru gives anyone a talk like this, it is a great motivator for intense introspection and change. I didn't leave my room for the next three days and spent that time analyzing Guru's words which remain indelibly printed on my heart. I prayed. I meditated. I discovered that, indeed, Guru was right—more than right. I saw that there was not a single action that I did without some expectation for an acknowledgment–a smile, a thank you or whatever. (And not only with Guru, but with everyone.) It was then that I made a promise. I was determined to become a "utility" student; that I would be happy no matter what; that

I would never doubt Guru's love for me; and that selflessness would become a theme for my life.

Well, Guru has an aphorism, "God has made my realisation easy. How I wish Him to make my nature's transformation easy also." It was easy to see the task at hand. It was easy to make a commitment to change. In fact, it was *not* easy to let go of my pride-attachment to that role.

When we returned home, Guru put me back on the massage role. The following year during the April Celebrations, Guru called me over to him. He told me that because I had been working hard, I should just relax during this celebration. Guru was being nice to me, but I was still not prepared for him not talking to me or not calling on me to work on him.

About a week into the celebration, I was in the throes of NOAMS when I walked into Lucille's Diner, a favourite local eatery in Queens. Ashrita happened to be there sitting at the counter with his head leaning a little sadly in his hand. I sat next to him and assumed the exact same position. Besides owning the most Guinness world records, Ashrita Furman, as I mentioned earlier, is Guru's main message-giver and probably spoke to Guru two to three times a day.

Anyway, we were both sitting at the counter, a little mopey, heads leaning on our hands, when I turned to Ashrita and asked, "Ashrita, is Guru upset with me? He hasn't spoken to me this entire celebration."

Ashrita assured me with his typical enthusiasm, "Nah, are you kidding? No way!"

"Are you sure?" I asked, and he reassured me. There was silence again.

A few moments of silence passed and Ashrita turned to me and asked, "Pradhan, is Guru upset with me? He hasn't spoken to me either!"

And I assured him with the same enthusiasm he showed me only a minute before, "Of course not!"

Of course, a moment later we looked at each other and started to laugh. Here we were both suffering from the same disease, the classic NOAMS. Realising this, I recommitted to becoming that utility student.

Well, the process took years. Every time I saw Guru, I would do so with the anticipation of working on him. And every time I wasn't asked, I would feel a little jealous, insecure and unhappy that someone else was performing the task. But I was fighting that feeling, so it bothered me a little less and less each time it happened.

A real resolution did not come until our visit to Thailand many years later. We were in the city of Chiang Mai, meeting in a room provided by a hotel different from where we were actually staying. I had been in a pretty good consciousness and felt that I had earned a trip to Guru's feet. Then it happened. Guru asked a brand new person to work on his legs. I was quite tired, and when I'm tired the wrong forces have an easy go of it, and they attacked me without mercy. I became upset and close to angry! Recognizing this pattern for what it was, I left the meeting room for my hotel room and decided it best to sleep it off with a nap.

Fortunately, when I awoke, I did so with some inspiration. I remembered my promise to be unconditional. I decided that I had to know what it was to love God selflessly, and so I sat down to meditate with the full determination to stay there until I could feel an iota of selfless love for God.

It didn't take long before I discovered that I had no idea how to love God unconditionally—absolutely no idea. I had only one recourse. I invited, I begged, I pleaded for God to enter into me to show me how to love Him selflessly. I don't know what happened or how, whether it was imagined or real, but I felt God enter into me with an overwhelming love. That's all that there was—an emanation of love. With that, suddenly and clearly I heard a distinct message in Guru's voice saying, "Why do you want to settle for my feet when I want to give you my heart?" A smile came to my face that was so broad it almost ached.

I cannot say how long I was there, but after some time I was inspired to go back to the meeting place. When I walked in, Guru was just preparing to leave. Everyone was standing, anticipating Guru's departure. Guru was still seated and reached for a few last cashews as he was about to rise from his chair. He glanced up at me for just a moment as I arrived. He asked, "Oh Pradhan, why are you smiling?" He did not look at me again.

"I'm smiling because..." I hesitated a moment.

Guru repeated without looking, "Yes, why are you smiling?"

"I'm smiling because I know that you love me." Both the boys and girls let out a collective "aw..." but they were of distinctively different tones—the boys a bit mocking, the girls more empathetic.

"I love you?" he asked, still not looking at me, still casually noshing on cashews.

"Yes," I affirmed. "You love me."

Without ever looking up at me, and ever so firmly he said, "Fine. I love you. Now, remember this for Eternity."

With that, I was released from my attachment. May I be blessed to remember this message forever.

⊙"Just who am I working on?"

Occasionally I had the opportunity to be with Guru alone in his home. On these rare occasions, I tried especially hard not to "pull" on him, so that he could relax, rest, or do whatever he wanted to.

On this particular occasion, Guru was on the massage table face down. He made a pillow of his arms and was in a light sleep. Now, a spiritual Master's sleep is different than typical sleep in the way you or I might do. What seems to happen—and this is totally my interpretation—is that the body is allowed to sleep while the Master travels off into some other plane of consciousness. This was certainly true for Guru. The evidence of this is that when Guru would eventually wake from a rest, he was aware of what that took place around him while he was sleeping.

So here I am sitting at Guru's feet, massaging him lightly because he seemed to be resting. I could see from Guru's slightly opened eyes that he was clearly in some meditative world. Something compelled me to break my intention to not bother Guru with questions. "Guru, may I ask you a question?"

With a voice that wasn't quite his, he acknowledged "Hmm." This was a yes.

"Guru," I said, "sometimes you invite me to massage you, and I know I am not in the best consciousness, and I'm certain that you will feel much worse when I am done. Does this ever bother you?"

With a voice that can only be described as coming from another world altogether came his reply, "Nothing touches me, nothing touches me."

I had the thought, "God, just who am I working on?"

⊙ I am your Eternity's father

When my father passed away, it was not completely unexpected. He had already experienced five heart attacks and two bouts of congestive heart failure. It was March 17, 1978 at around 10 a.m., when my younger brother called me from New York with the news. I immediately made two phone calls. The first call was to my dear friend, Ashrita, and I asked him to kindly inform Guru about my father's passing. The second call was to make a flight reservation.

To my surprise, within an hour or so, I received a call back from Ashrita. He informed me that Guru said upon my arrival in New York, I should come to his home, and to please bring a photo of my father. Guru added that I could come any time until 2 a.m. (Guru used a photo as a vehicle to access "the soul" of that individual. We, as seekers, will often speak of the soul as a theoretical concept, but for genuine spiritual Masters, the soul is absolutely real. Guru often said that he could see the soul as "more real" or "more clearly" than our physical.)

My father's passing occurred at a time in my life when I felt a little shaky, spiritually speaking. I was just opening my chiropractic office and spending a lot of money in the process. Perhaps my meditation time was sacrificed a bit as all this was happening. The net effect was that I wasn't feeling particularly good about myself spiritually.

As a result of this, I was not exactly prepared to stand in front of Guru. I must add that this is a completely wrong attitude. I've learned this since. There is perhaps no more important time to stand in front of your spiritual Teacher as when you are feeling least worthy. But that was not my wisdom at the time of this significant occurrence.

My flight arrived late in the evening, around 11 p.m. I made my way to Hartsdale where my brother lived with my father, showered and drove down to Guru's home in Jamaica, N.Y. It was

1 a.m. when I finally found myself standing on the street in front of Guru's home. The lights were off for the most part.

I stood there for a few minutes with a photo of my father affectionately surrounded by his four sons (see following page). It was clear which one was my father, both from an age stand-point and also from a focal standpoint. He was clearly the source of all the family vanity.

At this point, all my insecurity came forward. I knew I wasn't in a particularly good consciousness. I thought to myself, "Gee, the lights are out. Maybe I should go home, get in a decent morning meditation and then come back." This way, I could tell Guru that I was actually there but, because the lights were out, I didn't want to bother him. Very fortunately, my stupidity was corrected by another thought, "Your father has passed away. For God's sake, this is for him, not for you!"

I gathered my courage and went to the side door and knocked very gently, and I mean very, very gently. I thought that if no one answered, I could definitely go home and be able to tell Guru the next day, "I even knocked!" There was no answer.

If I knocked a second time with no answer, I would be fully justified in leaving. I knocked again, this time a bit harder. With that, the light came on, the door at the top of the stairs opened, and I could see Guru looking out at me.

I could hear him as he descended the steps, "Oh, I am so sorry good boy, so sorry." Then as he opened the door, he asked, "Did you bring a picture?"

"Yes, Guru," I said as I handed him the picture, feeling it needed no further explanation, as anyone would know which of the five men was my father.

I was so surprised when Guru asked, "Which one is it?"

I shrugged off my surprise and simply pointed to the man in the centre of the photo. "This one," I clarified.

My father surrounded by his four sons.
Clockwise from top left: Lenny, Jackie, Billy and myself (1975).

"Which one?" again Guru asked.

"This one," I said with a bit more emphasis.

"Which one?"

"This one!"

"Which one?"

"This one!!"

"Which one?"

At this point, I no longer understood why it wasn't obvious. Then the thought occurred to me that perhaps Guru had received a message that my brother had died and this was the source of his confusion. With that, I finally clarified it.

"This one, Guru. That's my father!"

At long last, it became all clear. With his eyes closed, soulfully, lovingly and softly, Guru repeated over and over, "I am your

Eternity's father. I am your Eternity's father. I am your Eternity's father. I am your Eternity's father. I am your Eternity's father." Perhaps twenty times he said it and, with each utterance, all my inner insecurity-angst dissipated to be replaced with my Guru's unvanquishable love. Then he opened his eyes and said, "I will do everything for your father that I can."

As I was leaving, he put the porch lights on and waved and smiled at me most compassionately and lovingly. It was a smile I will never forget.

⊙ Two fathers

I am always fond of saying that I have two fathers: Irving (along with Mum Beatrice) who parented Sandy, and Guru who gave birth to Pradhan. Well, the day after my father's passing and the late-night encounter with Guru, I received a message at my home, this time from Savyasachi, one of Guru's main assistants. "Guru said your father was extremely receptive and that he wants to hold a special meditation for your father tomorrow night."

I was surprised and delighted. Both my older brother Lenny and I attended this special meditation. It was an unusual meditation, to say the least. Guru called me up and had me sit in front of him. He told me to sit as close as possible and he asked me to remove my glasses! And then he meditated most powerfully. At a certain point, he placed his hand on my head and with his thumb massaged my third eye. (That point located between the eyebrows, a little above, is referred to as the "third eye". It is a spiritual centre for inner vision.) It was a most unique meditation and experience.

Afterwards, he commented, "Sandy's father's soul was sitting right next to him, most devoted, most soulfully. He was playing a musical instrument most effusively. I don't know if he played any instrument in this lifetime, but here he was definitely

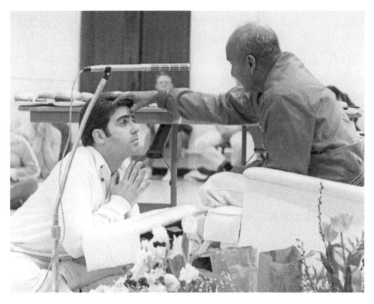

At the special meditation held for my father

playing with utmost devotion." (Again, recall my earlier comment that for Guru, the soul is absolutely real, accessible and
visible.)

I was struck by two things. One was the word "effusively".
I could only imagine what that meant, having never heard it
before. The second was this—I had been Pradhan for two years
or so at this point. Yet when Guru referred to my earthly dad, he
said "Sandy's father..."

I am grateful for both of my fathers.

○ Your father was here

I can always invoke a sense of my father. During the time subsequent to my mother's passing, he and I grew closer than the closest. It's hard to imagine any father and son being more inwardly close than we were.

A few years following my father's passing, I was on Guru's porch with about 30 others. It was my birthday, although nothing was said about celebrating it. Finally, as the last event of the evening, a birthday cake was brought out and handed to Guru, and Guru started to speak. I folded my hands assuming it was my birthday cake (which it was), but I began to doubt it when I heard what Guru was saying.

Although I can't remember his precise words, I do remember that the words were so flattering that I began to doubt that the birthday cake was for me. In fact, at a certain point, very slyly, I looked around to see if anyone else was sitting nearby with their hands expectantly folded as if it were their birthday! Whatever words Guru was saying were so flattering they couldn't possibly belong to me. It wasn't until Guru started singing "Happy Birthday" and I heard my name that I was convinced.

Wow!

Anyway, afterwards the conversation with Guru became casual. "Do you remember when I gave you your first interview on this porch?"

"Yes, Guru."

"You do? Okay, what colour pants were you wearing?"

I shrugged.

"Green!" he said, "and you were carrying something in your hand."

I started telling stories about the early days with my parents and how they reacted differently—how my mother temporarily disowned me and how my father became quite receptive.

"Yes, your father was quite receptive," Guru affirmed with a look that made me suspicious.

I inquired about my father, "Guru, does my father's soul ever appear before you? I mean, does he ever come to you?"

There was a moment's pause and then with a sheepish grin on his face, he explained, "Why do you think I said all these nice things in front of you? Because he was here! Inwardly, I could have communicated it with your soul and his soul, but because it made him feel a little proud to see his son flattered in front of all these other people, I said these things out loud!"

If you liked this selection of stories, you may order the entire book of stories at Amazon *(Go to Amazon and search for Pradhan Balter)*; or you can purchase it directly from me for a little less *(www.atthefeetofmymaster.com)*. This latter method has two advantages—first, it saves you a little money and second, it gives us the chance to meet or chat!

In closing...

In closing, please allow me to offer my gratitude to all of you who have taken the time to read this book, and to my many friends who have encouraged me to write it.

From the depths of my heart, I thank you. If ever I may be of service to anyone, I would be most grateful for that opportunity.

Finally, allow me to offer my gratitude to Sri Chinmoy, without whose love and compassionate nurturing I would have nothing to say.

For your first week's task...

Take a few minutes to quietly consider those qualities which give your life meaning or value. List seven such qualities:

1) . . . .

2) . . . .

3) . . . .

4) . . . .

5) . . . .

6) . . . .

7) . . . .

On each day of the week, meditate at least twice a day:

- five minutes first thing in the morning and;
- five minutes before you go to bed.

Each day, take one of the qualities and simply allow yourself to dwell in that quality during your meditation. Then throughout the day, try to appreciate (inwardly) that quality in others.

MON	☐ Morning meditation	☐ Evening meditation
TUE	☐ Morning meditation	☐ Evening meditation
WED	☐ Morning meditation	☐ Evening meditation
THU	☐ Morning meditation	☐ Evening meditation
FRI	☐ Morning meditation	☐ Evening meditation
SAT	☐ Morning meditation	☐ Evening meditation
SUN	☐ Morning meditation	☐ Evening meditation

AUM

"*AUM is the soundless sound. It is the vibration of the Supreme. It is called the Seed-Sound of the Universe, for with this sound, the Supreme set into motion the first vibration of His creation. The teeming universe is sustained perpetually by the creative vibration of the Divine AUM.*

The syllable AUM is indivisible, but each portion of it represents a different aspect of the Supreme. The Sanskrit A represents and embodies the Consciousness of the Creator, Brahma; the Sanskrit U, the Preserver, Vishnu; the Sanskrit M, the Transformer, Shiva. Taken together, AUM is the spontaneous cosmic rhythm with which God embraces the universe.

The universal AUM, put forth by the Supreme, is an infinite Ocean. The individual AUM, chanted by man, is a drop in that Ocean. It cannot be separated from the Ocean but, nevertheless, even the tiniest drop can claim the Ocean as its very own. Chanting AUM, man touches and calls forth the cosmic vibration of the Supreme Sound. When one can hear the Soundless Sound within oneself, when one can identify oneself with it, when one can live within the AUM, one can be freed from the fetters of ignorance and realise the Supreme within and without.

The unknown embraces ignorance with its self-limitation. The unknowable embraces AUM with His absolute Self-revelation.

Without birth is the Supreme; without birth is AUM. Without end is the Supreme; without end is AUM. Immortality is AUM's universal Identity.

When we are in ignorance, AUM feeds us, for AUM is God. When we are in Knowledge, AUM still feeds us. When we are beyond both ignorance and Knowledge, AUM continues to feed us, for it is the nectar which gives life to creation, born and unborn.

(by Sri Chinmoy, 'AUM' magazine, 1965)

Book references

In case you are inspired to read more, these are the books by Sri Chinmoy from which I have quoted the poems, aphorisms and prose throughout the book (in alphabetical order).

A God-Lover's Earth-Heaven-Life, Part 1, New York: Agni Press, 1974.

A Heart of Oneness-Peace, New York: Agni Press, 1999.

Aspiration-Tree, Agni Press: 1976.

Colour Kingdom, "Transformation", New York: AUM Publications, 1973.

Consciousness: God-Journey to Man; Man-Journey to God, "Consciousness–Light", New York: Sri Chinmoy Lighthouse, 1974.

Death and Reincarnation, New York: AUM Publication, 1997.

Eternity's Breath, New York: Sri Chinmoy Lighthouse, 1972.

Fifty Freedom-Boats to One Golden Shore, Part 6, New York: Agni Press, 1975.

I Need This Book, "Action", New York: Agni Press, 1992.

My Christmas-New Year-Vacation-Aspiration-Prayers, Part 15, New York: Agni Press, 2003.

My Christmas-New Year-Vacation-Aspiration-Prayers, Part 16, New York: Agni Press, 2003.

My Christmas-New Year-Vacation-Aspiration-Prayers, Part 3, New York: Agni Press, 2000.

My Heart's Peace-Offering, "Concentration", New York: Agni Press, 1994.

My Heart's Thirty-One Sacred Secret, New York: Agni Press, 1982.

My Lord's Secrets Revealed, Herder and Herder, 1971; Reprinted by Agni Press, 1984.

My Maple Tree, Agni Press: 1974.

My Rose Petals, Part 5, New York: Agni Press, 1976.

New Year's Messages from Sri Chinmoy: 1966-2007, "1968", New York: Aum Publications, 2010.

Peace-Blossom-Fragrance, Part 1, New York: Agni Press, 1994.

Philosopher-Thinkers: The Power-Towers of the Mind and *Poet-Seers: The Fragrance-Hours of the Heart in the West*, New York: Agni Press, 1998.

Poetry: My Rainbow-Heart-Dreams, New York: Agni Press, 1993.

Rainbow-Flowers, Part 1, "Tolerance", New York: Agni Press, 1973. Reprinted by New York: Sri Chinmoy Lighthouse, 1974.

Seventy-Seven Thousand Service-Trees, New York: Agni Press, 2004.

Silence-Seed and Sound-Fruit, New York: Agni Press, 1975.

Silver Thought-Waves, Part 1, "Duty", New York: Agni Press, 1992.

Songs of the Soul, New York: Herder and Herder, 1971. Reprinted, New York: Agni Press, 1983.

Ten Thousand Flower-Flames, Part 10, New York: Agni Press, 1981.

Ten Thousand Flower-Flames, Part 100, New York: Agni Press, 1983.

Ten Thousand Flower-Flames, Part 12, New York: Agni Press, 1981.

Ten Thousand Flower-Flames, Part 19, New York: Agni Press, 1981.

Ten Thousand Flower-Flames, Part 21, New York: Agni Press, 1981.

Ten Thousand Flower-Flames, Part 32, New York: Agni Press, 1982.

Ten Thousand Flower-Flames, Part 34, New York: Agni Press, 1982.

Ten Thousand Flower-Flames, Part 40, New York: Agni Press, 1982.

Ten Thousand Flower-Flames, Part 41, New York: Agni Press, 1982.

Ten Thousand Flower-Flames, Part 80, New York: Agni Press, 1983.

The Dance of Life, Part 13, #650, New York: Agni Press, 1973.

The Garland of Nation-Souls, Deerfield Beach, Fla.: Health Communications, Inc., 1995.

The Height Of Silence And The Might Of Sound, New York: AUM Publications.

The Inner Role of the United Nations, Zurich: Madal Bal, 1993.

The Silence-Song, "Consciousness", New York: Agni Press, 1975.

The Silent Teaching, Edinburgh, Scotland: Sri Chinmoy Centre, 1981.

The Summits of God-Life: Samadhi and Siddhi, New York: AUM Publications, 1999.

The Vision-Sky of California, "Music", New York: Agni Press, 1980.

The Wings of Light, Part 19, New York: Agni Press, 1974.

Transcendence-Perfection, New York: Agni Press, 1975. Reprinted 2009.

Wings of Joy, New York: Simon and Schuster, 1997.

Yoga and the Spiritual Life, New York: Agni Press, 1974.

You Are Your Life's Progress-Joy-Drum, New York: Agni Press, 1993.

Latest books by Sri Chinmoy

The Adventure of Life:
On Yoga, meditation, and the art of living

A modern-day spiritual manual that encourages the reader to embrace new ideas, adding a deeper, spiritual dimension to one's life. In a clear and accessible way, Sri Chinmoy speaks about the spiritual art of living, society and religion as well as popular topics such as chakras, occult powers and the end of the world, and introduces us to a modern spiritual lifestyle with focus on health, diet, sport, family life and the workplace. (*www.lifeadventure.net*)

222 Meditation Techniques

These 222 guided exercises, the largest collection of meditation techniques in one book, are suitable for both beginners and advanced seekers who wish to explore the world of meditation. From breathing exercises, guided meditations and the use of mantras, to special exercises for runners, artists and musicians, ways to overcome depression, stress and bad habits, and even losing weight, this book offers a truly broad canvas of possibilities. (*www.themeditationbook.net*)

Sport & Meditation:
The Inner Dimension of Sport

This is a unique book, which challenges our preconceptions of our physical capacities and of the limitations of age. It includes specific exercises concerning meditation, concentration and mantra as aids to the focus needed in all forms of exercise and training. It is this new facet that enables us to achieve peak performance, to get more from exercise and to enjoy robust and lasting health and wellbeing.

World champions such as Carl Lewis, Tatyana Lebedeva, Tegla Loroupe, Bill Pearl, and Paul Tergat share their own inner secrets and spiritual perspectives on training and competition in anecdotes peppered throughout the book.
(*www.sportandmeditation.com*)

Heart-Wisdom-Drops
Inspiring Aphorisms for Every Day

This collection of 55 inspirational cards makes an excellent gift. Each card features an aphorism and meditative painting by Sri Chinmoy. For those seeking hope, peace of mind and life-wisdom these cards offer inspiration, and are a guide to a happy, harmonious and spiritually-grounded daily life.
(*www.wisdom-cards.com*)

For more books kindly visit *www.bluebeyondbooks.co.uk.*

About the author

Pradhan Balter is a chiropractor, a computer consultant, and owns a vegetarian restaurant and flower store in Chicago. Perhaps more relevant to this book, he has studied meditation for some 45 years with Indian spiritual Teacher Sri Chinmoy. Pradhan serves as director of the Chicago Sri Chinmoy Centre, and has lectured across the United States and in some 40 countries abroad.

Pradhan is available to speak to groups of any size about meditation. His down-to-earth style and light-hearted approach make meditation both accessible and inspiring. There is never a charge, nor are donations ever accepted for such events.

Contact Pradhan...
e-mail: pradhan@pradhanb.com
address: Pradhan Balter
            2135 W. Roscoe St-1S
            Chicago, IL 60618
            U.S.A.
web: www.a21stcenturyseeker.com